READY

OR

NOT

PAM
PARISH

PRAISE FOR *READY OR NOT*

Book One in the Ready or Not Series for Foster & Adoptive Families

Anyone considering foster care or adoption should first spend 30 days with this book. As foster parents ourselves, we've found *Ready or Not* to be a valuable tool on our journey. So much so, that it's now a part of the core curriculum for families desiring to foster or adopt in our churches. Pam's transparency throughout the book gives a realistic picture of what to expect. Her Biblical insights powerfully draw us to the heart of God and His love for orphaned and at-risk children.
Andy and Sandra Stanley, *North Point Community Church*

In this thought provoking biblical study, Pam Parish clearly captures the journey of adoption and foster care. The experience brings parental transformation. Of critical importance for every perspective adoptive parent is to count the cost. *Ready or Not* does just that. This is an excellent resource for faith-based adoption and foster care agencies to use as well as adoption ministries within the local church. I highly recommend it!
Jayne Schooler, Co-author of *Wounded Children, Healing Homes* and *The Whole Life Adoption Book*

Foster care and adoption are beautiful. They are also full of brokenness. Potential parents need to be equipped and aware of the realities of adopting children that come from hard places. Pam Parish shares stories of her own personal journey as well as keen wisdom and biblical insight in *Ready or Not*. I will be recommending this book to every person that is considering foster care and adoption. *Ready or Not* will be an invaluable tool to help them determine if God is calling them to this journey.
Johnny Carr, Author of *Orphan Justice*

My wife and I have been leading a small group at our local church that is focused on prospective and current adoptive and foster parents. It was a huge blessing to take 6 weeks to focus on the *Ready or Not* study!

This is one of the best resources I've found to count the costs of adopting and fostering, while at the same time creating a supportive team to hold each other up throughout their journeys. Each week, the probing questions led to deep discussions and honest reflection, calling each of us to consider what unconditional love truly looks like in action. As a result of this study, I believe our group members have united as a community of believers to stand together through thick and thin and to trust the Lord as He sets the lonely in their families. Thank you so much for providing this valuable resource to families considering fostering and adoption!

David Hennessey, Director for Global Movements
Christian Alliance for Orphans (CAFO)

Every prospective foster and adoptive parent should be given this book in advance of receiving a child into their home. Pam speaks with such truth, passion and understanding of the journey with a child who comes from a hard place. As a foster and adoptive parent, how I wish we could have had such a resource in the beginning of our journey. This is a MUST read for those considering the decision to foster or adopt.

Ruby Johnston, Co-Founder, *LAMb International*

In Pam Parish's book, *Ready or Not*, Pam challenges us to consider God's heart for orphans and our specific role in aligning our heart with His. This 30-day journey will inspire you through Pam's honest and heartfelt words and through Scriptures that confirmed her calling. It will recalibrate your expectations and motivation as you enter into your own calling. It will affirm your daily journey with God as He leads you on an adventure that will draw you into His intimacy for you and the broken.

Mary Frances Bowley
Founder, Wellspring Living
Author of *A League of Dangerous Women* **and** *The White Umbrella*

It is a privilege to call Pam a friend and I am so excited for others to hear what God has placed in her heart for parents and families! *Ready or Not* is not only an encouraging resource on adoption and foster care. But it is a tremendous sharing of life experiences and strategic scripture verses for such an incredible faith journey.

God is doing a mighty new thing in the church for children and families! He is using powerful testimonies and those that are willing to serve to impact precious lives for His glory. So as you read this book, prepare to be challenged. Expect the Lord's divine ministry. Then be available to be immersed deeper in His love and walk in obedience. Get ready!

Jordan Palser, *Orphan's Promise*

When I first began my journey toward becoming a foster mom I was full of enthusiasm and, what I believed to be, exceptional preparation. I had nearly finished raising my own five children and the training that I received from my faith based agency seemed comprehensive. It took a lot of time, so it certainly didn't occur to me to question it. What I discovered after taking my first placement was that the emotional and spiritual preparation was completely inadequate. Where insights, that can only be given by an experienced person who has traveled the road before you belonged, there was nothing. This devotional is truly inspired. When I first read it I realized it needed to be an essential part of the preparation for all foster, respite or pre-adoptive families in our church's ministry. It is challenging but life-giving all at the same time. I could, and do, return to it over and over again for insight, comfort and inspiration. Thank you, Pam, for following the prompting that led to *Ready Or Not!*
Lesli Reece, Ministry Director—Fostering Together
North Point Ministries, Inc.

When transitioning from respite foster parenting to full-time foster parenting, my husband and I decided to prepare by going through this devotional together each morning. Even in the first days, the material started to slowly help us break through some surface level emotions and uncover hidden fears and reservations we weren't aware we harbored. The poignant and honest examples followed by penetrating questions, raised issues that lurked in the backs of our minds that we'd never verbalized.

Although we'd done the initial foster parent training followed by several trainings on behavior and discipline, nothing has prepared us for the challenges of fostering like this devotional. As a couple we've been able to honestly reveal our fears, joys and reservations about fostering. *Ready or Not* has opened the door for continuing conversations. If it were up to us, we would say, "Do not start fostering until you've done this devotional together." No 30 days could be better spent to prepare you for the adventure ahead.
Johnna Stein, Director of Ministry Development, *Promise 686*

Ready or Not

30-Day Discovery For Families Growing Through Foster Care & Adoption

*Book One in the Ready or Not Series
for Foster & Adoptive Families*

Written By:
Pam Parish

Foreword By:
Sandra Stanley

Editors: Dan Mancini, Kristan Parish
Cover Art: Big Stock Photography
Cover Design: Steve Parish
Author Photo: Craig Obrist Photography
Inspiration: Every foster and adoptive family that I've ever met.

ISBN: 0692217940
ISBN-13: 978-0692217948

DEDICATION

No one deserves more honor in the writing of this prayer journal than my Lord and Savior Jesus Christ, without whom I am nothing. To my husband and best friend, Steve: *thank you* for loving and leading me. To my wonderful daughters: you've taught us how to be better people. I'm so honored you call me mom.

CONTENTS

ACKNOWLEDGMENTS

I want to thank my husband, Steve, for always being my rock and for believing I can do anything I put my mind to. I will never have a better person in my corner than you. To my daughters, Katya Grace, Kelsey Joy, Seara Serenity, Elizabeth Yeaune Harang, Charlie Selah, Kristan Faith, and Heather Hope: you are the lights of my life. Thank you for teaching me patience, understanding, laughter, and love.

To our parents'—Gary & Janice Parish, Wayne Gary, Yvonne Marcus— and all of our extended family: you've watched our family grow in extraordinary ways and have accepted each change and new addition with unconditional love. You amaze me.

To our pastors, Dennis and Colleen Rouse: I've learned how to follow Jesus, hear His voice, and walk in obedience because of your uncompromising teaching and example. I love you and am so thankful to be a part of Victory World Church. God chose to sow the seeds of orphan care in my heart here. Since I first stepped foot into Victory, my life has been a journey of moving from *"success to significance."*

To my friend and agent, Ryan Howard: your encouragement, advice and direction have been priceless. I'm honored to work with you on this project and others to come. I'm so glad that we crossed paths with you and Christi over duck wraps at Cotton!

To the Promise 686 & 111 Initiative team: this entire project would still be sitting on my website if it weren't for you. Tim and Amy Rider, Andy Cook, Johnna Stein, Ken Reed, David & Lisa Hennessey and Tracy Baird: "thank you" isn't sufficient.

To the North Point Ministries Team: you have believed in and invested in this project and me in unbelievable ways. Lesli Reece, I love that you're my friend. Thank you for implementing this content into Fostering Together's equipping environment and leading the way in pushing me to get it out as a resource to others. Sandra Stanley, your belief in this project is humbling. I'm forever grateful for your friendship, encouragement and support. Suzy Gray, I count myself eternally grateful to know you. Thank you for giving me your precious time throughout this project. This book is available to others because you made yourself available to me. Dan Mancini, wow. I so appreciate your help in the copy editing and discussion questions for each day. The sheer fact that you endured 30 days of my addiction to run-on sentences deserves to be recognized.

To Daniel Homrich, Joe Kissack and Laura Engelbrecht: the three of you have played a huge role in this book getting here. Daniel, your friendship has meant the world to me over this last year. Thank you for dreaming with me, challenging me and strategizing with me. Joe, for as long as I live, I will never forget the first time I met you. You walked into the room and said, "I love it!!!! I read the WHOLE thing last night!" Thank you so much for that memory. Laura, you have to be one of the most encouraging people that I've ever known. My spirit feels cared for when I'm with you. To me, that's priceless.

Gary and Paula Walderich: I am so thankful that God brought you into my life. You are amazing. Thank you for always being in my corner to encourage, challenge and take care of me. Your role in my life is much deeper than friends, you're family. I love you both so much.

To our community of friends, Montell and Kristin Jordan, Kyle and Mallory Cruz, Kyle and Jess Purintin, Nathan and Ashley Williams, Charlie and Erin Pike, and Chad and Beth Whiteside: thank you for doing life with us. I can't tell you how much your friendship and love means to our family. We're so blessed to walk through our celebrations and trials with you. We love you so very much.

Thank you to the many others who have been an inspiration throughout this project. Michael Buckingham, thank you for helping me make the title better. Your early morning epiphany was just what was needed. Nick and Susan Gage, you are two of the most committed foster parents that I've ever known. It's a privilege to call you friends. Thank you for modeling unconditional love to your community and kids.

To all of our Victory World Church family: we are blessed to have you in our lives. You've loved each of our girls, mentored them, cried with them, corrected them, and laughed with them as if they were your own. We are eternally grateful.

To Bethany Christian Services and the many counselors, social workers, adoption experts, families and friends along the way: your insight, calming direction, and understanding have been invaluable.

For I know the plans I have for you, says the Lord.

Plans to prosper you and not harm you, plans to give you

HOPE AND A FUTURE

Jeremiah 29:11

INTRODUCTION

"Hope and a future." There's so much promise packed into those four little words. Jeremiah 29:11 has been my life verse for nearly two decades. I grabbed hold of it early in my walk with the Lord. He's been faithful to those words in my life on countless occasions. It was God's promise to *me*. I trusted Him. Because of this one little verse, I've always known that nothing I go through will ultimately harm me. This trust has given me the strength to continue through many difficult circumstances.

As a potential adoptive parent, I came face-to-face with those words in a totally different light. This same "hope and a future" that God had promised me is what I am potentially promising a child I've never met, don't know, and won't meet for quite some time. Just as He, my heavenly Father, promises no harm will come to me and through Him I now have a hope and a future, I now make that same promise to a child. *Am I ready for all that means?*

For my husband and me, the journey into adoptive parenting began with a desire to add to our family. We didn't have a big spiritual revelation or instructions from God. We just wanted another child. Since our daughter, Kristan, was eleven when we decided to adopt, older child adoption made the most sense for us. Although our decision wasn't based solely on a "word from God," we instinctively knew it was a serious and spiritual one. We knew once we committed to a child, it was for a lifetime, no matter what happened. We had no idea how much and how often that commitment would be challenged.

I stepped into adoptive parenting blind. I didn't know anyone who had adopted children out of foster care. I didn't even know anyone who had fostered children. I only knew that we wanted to add a daughter to our family, and that Kristan was tired of being an only child and wanted a sister. I am thankful for that blindness because I'm certain that if God had told me then how my life would look in seven years, I would have run . . . far and fast. During our adoption journey, I learned many lessons about parenting and unconditional love. I learned that when God asks you to do something, He's wise in revealing how to do it one step at a time.

As you step into foster or adoptive parenting for the first time, there's no way to see the end. But I'm convinced there are things you can do to prepare your heart in partnership with God for this new gift of forever family. God gave my family supernatural grace along the way. Thanks to His forever faithfulness and a great community, we made it through some tremendously difficult times. Some families' stories don't turn out that way. I have seen foster and adoptive placements fail. People set out on their journeys with good intentions, but good intentions aren't enough to sustain you during the tough times. You need a plan.

Maybe you've watched a friend foster or adopt and they made it look fulfilling and easy. Maybe you've seen an emotional presentation with pictures of dozens of gorgeous children in need of "healing homes" and "forever family." Maybe you're struggling with the agony of childlessness because of infertility. Whatever your reason for considering foster care or adoption, thank you. These precious girls and boys need people like you to answer the call to give them a hope and a future.

For better or for worse, adoption is a lifetime commitment. Foster care is a commitment to loving a wounded child. It's a massive undertaking. *Ready or Not* is a resource designed to help you take the next thirty days to prayerfully consider your decision. My prayer is that it will challenge your heart and commitment, and encourage you to ask the hard questions and think about the tough times. It is also my prayer that you will discover in God the heart of a father to the fatherless and allow His love to burn deeply in your heart. His plans for you are good.

Ready or not . . . here we go.

Pam Parish

Discussion Questions – Introduction

1. Have you watched a friend or family member go through adoption or foster care? What are your impressions of their experience?

2. As this study begins, you're encouraged to take thirty days to prayerfully consider your decision. Why do you think Pam says it's wise to take this time? What do you expect to discover?

3. Read Jeremiah 29:11. How does God's promise make you feel? What do you think it means in the context of being the parent who is promising "hope and a future" to a child?

4. What are you currently asking God to do as He prepares your heart for becoming a foster or adoptive parent? How can this group pray for you?

HOW TO USE THIS 30-DAY JOURNAL

TOGETHER

I've written this journal with couples and friends in mind because any journey is easier when there's someone else linking arms with you. If you're married, walk through the thirty days with your spouse. If you're a single parent, find a trusted friend who will challenge you, encourage you, and who isn't afraid to help you dig deep for the truth. You are going to need to rely on each other in your journey. Start now.

REPEATED THEMES

Although no two days of this study are exactly the same, you will see some repeated themes as we travel through the next thirty days. God's mandates regarding the orphan are repeated often in the Bible, so we will revisit them again and again. There are also common areas that cause families to falter and stall. I will repeat them in different ways to make sure you're thinking through potential challenges from every possible angle.

SCRIPTURE STUDY

Each day of *Ready or Not* includes a main scripture and scripture meditations. I encourage you to write down these verses in your personal journal and take time to meditate on them throughout the day. If there's one thing that's most important in this journey, it's the Word written on your heart so you remember it in difficult times. The Word will sustain you, encourage you, give you insight, and bring life and joy into your home. Take all the time you need to meditate on it so it roots deeply into your heart.

JOURNALING

You are going to experience a wide range of emotions, victories, and setbacks. Journaling is a great way to remember and celebrate God's faithfulness. You'll sometimes feel like you're *never* going to get through this challenge or *this* behavior is never going to end, but you will and they do. Being able to look back at the difficulties you've overcome will bring immense encouragement as you move forward.

PRAYER STARTERS

I've given you short prayer starters at the end of each day. These are simply my words—nothing special or sacred. Make them your own. Talk to God about the real stuff that's happening in your heart. This journey is an ongoing conversation between you and God. Be real. Be you. He knows anyway.

DISCUSSION QUESTIONS

At the end of each day, you'll find a set of questions designed to help you work through and apply the day's devotion. These can be discussed as a couple, in a small group setting, or with a trusted friend. I encourage you to take the time to discuss this material with someone else.

PLACE THESE WORDS ON YOUR HEARTS. GET THEM DEEP INSIDE YOU. TIE THEM

ON YOUR HANDS AND FOREHEADS AS A REMINDER. TEACH THEM TO YOUR

CHILDREN. TALK ABOUT THEM WHEREVER YOU ARE, SITTING AT HOME OR

WALKING IN THE STREET; TALK ABOUT THEM FROM THE TIME YOU GET UP IN

THE MORNING UNTIL YOU FALL INTO BED AT NIGHT. INSCRIBE THEM ON THE

DOORPOSTS AND GATES OF YOUR CITIES SO THAT YOU'LL LIVE A LONG TIME,

AND YOUR CHILDREN WITH YOU, ON THE SOIL THAT GOD PROMISED TO GIVE

YOUR ANCESTORS FOR AS LONG AS THERE IS A SKY OVER THE EARTH.

DEUTERONOMY 11:18-21 (MSG)

FOREWORD

It took three years, but she finally opened up. Her words tumbled out without order or eloquence. She shared what life had been like before the only normal she knew was snatched away. She shared stories of fear. She shared stories of hunger and neglect. The days had been rocky at best, but they were familiar. The idea of that familiarity being replaced by the uncertainty of foster care was far more frightening.

But, God. God saw her in her hours of need. He placed her in a safe home. He introduced her to Himself. Three years later, she was finally able to muster enough courage, enough trust. She was able to rest. She was able to see that God had a plan all along. And she was able to share her story.

Will everything now be perfect, and seamless, and joy filled? Certainly not. However, some wounds have been healed. Some lies have been replaced with truth. Where the dead ends were, there is now a glimmer of hope.

That story is true. It's not only true in my experience as a foster mom, it's a frequently occurring true story. Both foster care and adoption have their unique challenges. That's why I'm so very grateful that Pam Parish has given us this amazing resource.

After being handed this manuscript by a mutual friend, I quickly discovered that Pam knows what she's talking about. She's adopted six beautiful girls "from hard places." She's acutely aware of the challenges and potential difficulties foster and adoptive parents face. Pam's devotional thoughts and insights continue to encourage me in my own foster mom journey. Ready or Not is also quickly becoming a vital tool for Fostering Together, our ministry to fostering and adopting families at North Point Ministries.

It takes more than a compassionate heart, an extra bed, and hours of training to be an effective foster parent. Foster and adoptive parents also need daily doses of encouragement to stay the course and make the necessary adjustments along the way. Ready or Not: 30-Day Discovery provides just that. Thank you, Pam!

Sandra Stanley

RELIGION THAT GOD OUR FATHER ACCEPTS AS PURE AND FAULTLESS IS THIS:

TO LOOK AFTER ORPHANS AND WIDOWS IN THEIR DISTRESS AND TO KEEP

ONESELF FROM BEING POLLUTED BY THE WORLD.

JAMES 1:27

DAY 1: THE CALL

Not many would debate whether God's will is for orphaned and wounded children, but few have fully considered it. In Psalm 68:5–6, God calls Himself a father to the fatherless and says that He sets the lonely into family. In James 1:27, it's clear that God sees caring for the orphan as pure and faultless. And in Psalm 127:3, we're told that children are a gift from the Lord, a reward from Him. There are many other scriptures we'll read throughout this thirty-day journey that emphasize God's heart for His people to answer the call of adoption. However, each believer must prayerfully consider his or her part in answering that call. For some, it means financial support to a family that is adopting, childcare assistance, making weekly meals for a family, helping with school clothes, or supporting an orphanage. Answering the call for you might mean committing to a child for life through adoption or walking with a child temporarily through foster care.

> **"Not many would debate whether God's will is for orphaned and wounded children, but few have fully considered it."**

In considering the call of James 1:27, many overlook the work of foster parenting because the children aren't 'orphans' in the truest sense of the

10

word. Children in foster care are probably best categorized as "at-risk" children from "at-risk" families. They have parents, but their parents aren't able to care for them in a stable, safe environment. Caring for children who've experienced the trauma of abuse and neglect is no small task; it takes boldness and courage. Foster parents have a unique opportunity to impact the lives of the children in their care for eternity. Whether a child is in your life for moments or years, you could potentially be the only reflection of Jesus that they ever encounter. Helping to reunite a family in crisis is a beautiful way to be the light of Jesus within the community.

It's clear that God's will is for all followers of Christ to take the gospel to the world, but that doesn't mean it's His will for everyone to pastor a church. In the same way, it's God's will that we care for orphans, but that doesn't mean every family is called to adopt. Too often, families confuse God's whisper to get involved in the cause of orphans as a directive to add an orphaned child to their family. That can lead to heartbreak for even the most well-intentioned family.

It's important that you take time to ask God to speak clearly to you about your specific and unique call to adoption. Our call is to older teenage girls. It's unique, it's specific, and it's what God has asked us to do. To others it might be adopting an infant domestically or internationally. Ask specifically. He'll answer.

Scripture Meditation: Take a few minutes to read the following scriptures. Allow the Holy Spirit to speak to your heart about each of them.

Psalm 68:5–6 (NLT) Father to the fatherless, defender of widows—this is God, whose dwelling is holy. God places the lonely in families; he sets the prisoners free and gives them joy. But he makes the rebellious live in a sun-scorched land.

Psalm 127:3 (NLT) Children are a gift from the Lord; they are a reward from him.

James 1:27 (NLT) Pure and genuine religion in the sight of God the Father means caring for orphans and widows in their distress and refusing to let the world corrupt you."

Capturing Thoughts: Throughout your adoption journey, I encourage you to capture your thoughts, fears, moments of joy, memories, and challenges. It will be a great encouragement to go back and read what you've written. You'll be surprised how much you and your family grow through your experiences.

Prayer Starter: Father, our hearts are broken for the children in our world that are without a family. We know you want us to help bridge the gaps for these kids. Would you show us your desire and how you would specifically guide us in this journey of caring for orphaned and at-risk children? We know that you can open doors no man can close and close those that no man can open. We trust you.

Discussion Questions - Day 1: The Call

1. What motivated you to get involved in foster care or adoption? Was it an emotional draw? Did you have an experience with a particular child or family?

2. Today's devotion says, "Caring for children who've experienced the trauma of abuse and neglect is no small task; it takes boldness and courage." Talk about what you think this would mean to you and your family.

3. Read Psalm 68:5-6. What do you think it means that God "sets the lonely in families"? What does it mean to your involvement in foster care?

4. What are you currently praying about related to your foster or adoption journey? How can this group pray for you?

My Journey:

(Use this space to capture your thoughts, prayers, concerns and questions

GREATER LOVE HAS NO ONE THAN THIS; TO LAY DOWN ONE'S LIFE

FOR ONE'S FRIENDS.

JOHN 15:13

DAY 2: LAY DOWN YOUR LIFE

When we hear the phrase "lay down your life," we automatically think of Jesus dying on the cross as a ransom for us. That truly is the ultimate sacrifice. But there's another powerful way to lay down one's life for friends. Jesus modeled it as well. He left all the comforts of glory to be born in a filthy stable to human parents, grow up as a carpenter's son, and walk the earth for three years of ministry under scrutiny, persecution, rejection, and betrayal.

As a foster or adoptive parent, you choose to lay down your life in dedicated service to another. Parenting itself is an act of sacrifice. We lay down our independence—our ability to go here and there, do this or that—to have children. When the sacrifice becomes too much with biological children, it's easy to keep going because there's no easy way of escape. With foster/adopted children, it's much harder because when it gets difficult our thoughts can betray us. After all, they aren't *our* children; we aren't the cause of their behavior. Something happened to them when they were young that we had no control over. We aren't cut out for this. We should send them

"When you leave the comforts of life as you know it to enter into life with a child who has been abandoned, rejected, hurt or abused, you enter into her brokenness."

back. Those are the moments that laying down your life becomes a reality, a choice you have to make.

Some of the darkest moments with my children have been the brightest moments in my life with Jesus. We aren't promised an absence of trouble in this life. Truthfully, we're promised the opposite – especially when we're pursuing the call of God. But we serve a God who is in the restoration and resurrection business. As we die to our expectations, we open our hearts to God's bigger plan. Meeting one of my children in the middle of their pain is messy. There have been moments that I've felt so totally ill-equipped and lost. At those times, when I've turned to Jesus with a deeply broken and insecure heart, He has always led me to grace, understanding and perseverance. Dying to myself allows the work of redemption to take place in its proper time.

When you leave the comforts of life as you know it to enter into life with a child who has been abandoned, rejected, hurt, or abused, you enter into her brokenness. When the child screams at you that you aren't her parent, what are you going to do? When the child breaks your dishes, writes on your walls, kicks and bites you, runs away or turns up high or pregnant, what are you going to do? Understanding clearly what God has called you to do will give you sustaining power in these moments. Ask Him to burn a supernatural love—a love like Jesus'—into your heart . . . starting now.

Scripture Meditation: Take a few moments to read the following scriptures. Allow the Holy Spirit to speak to your heart about each of them.

John 15:13 (NLT) There is no greater love than to lay down one's life for one's friends.

1 John 4:7-10 (NLT) Dear friends, let us continue to love one another, for love comes from God. Anyone who loves is a child of God and knows God. But anyone who does not love does not know God, for God is love. God showed how much he loved us by sending his one and only Son into the world so that we might have eternal life through him. This is real love – not that we loved God, but that he loved us and sent his Son as a sacrifice to take away our sins.

1 John 4:20 (NLT) If someone says, "I love God," but hates a Christian brother or sister, that person is a liar; for if we don't love people we can see, how can we love God, whom we cannot see?

Proverbs 18:24 (NLT) There are "friends" who destroy each other, but a real friend sticks closer than a brother.

1 John 3:16 (NLT) We know what real love is because Jesus gave up his life for us. So we also ought to give up our lives for our brothers and sisters.

Capturing Thoughts: Throughout your adoption journey, I encourage you to capture your thoughts, fears, moments of joy, memories, and challenges. It will be a great encouragement to go back and read what you've written. You'll be surprised how much you and your family grow through your experiences.

Prayer Starter: Father, we understand that your Word tells us the greatest love we can show others is to lay down our lives for them. Give us a heart like yours to enter into whatever mess our future children may have and lay down the comforts, doubts, and fears of our lives to serve them. Prepare our hearts for what only you know will come.

Discussion Questions – Day 2: Lay Down Your Life

1. Talk about a time in your life when you felt overwhelmed by the details because you couldn't see God's big picture. What happened? How did that experience change your relationship with God?

2. Read Jeremiah 29:11. Why is it sometimes challenging to believe that God has plans to give us a hope and a future?

3. How does the idea that God has plans and hopes for each foster or adoptive child change the way you view parents' responsibilities?

4. What is one thing you can do this week to open your heart and your life to the plans and hopes that God has for you? What can this group do to support you?

My Journey:

(Use this space to capture your thoughts, prayers, concerns and questions)

GOING A LITTLE FARTHER, HE FELL TO THE GROUND AND PRAYED THAT IF POSSIBLE THE HOUR MIGHT PASS FROM HIM. *"ABBA*, FATHER," HE SAID, "EVERYTHING IS POSSIBLE FOR YOU. TAKE THIS CUP FROM ME. YET NOT WHAT I WILL, BUT WHAT YOU WILL."

MARK 14:35-36

DAY 3: NOT MY WILL, BUT YOURS BE DONE

"You have to do what's best for you." That's a phrase that we've all heard and uttered many times. The problem is, it's wrong. What's best for us in our human reasoning is often the opposite of what God's will is for us in His divine plan. Given the choice, would any of us willingly accept cancer, purposely cut off a limb, or go to a brutal death on a cross for stuff we didn't even do? "What you think is best for you" is the wrong measure for life, much less for making the decision to become a foster or adoptive parent.

> **"'What you think is best for you' is the wrong measure for life, much less for making the decision to adopt a child."**

I remember a time when we faced a pretty significant issue with one of our daughters and had to make a tough decision. As we walked out the weeks following the decision, the scrutiny was sometimes unbearable. Some people understood and completely supported our decision; others thought we were wrong. Walking in between opposing opinions was difficult, and we knew there were multiple ways that the situation could ultimately end. The supporting messages were as loud as the opposing ones, *"You have to do what's best for your entire family." "You've done all you can do, now it's up to her." "She just doesn't appreciate what you're trying to do for her.", "Just let her go, you tried to make family for her, if she doesn't want that – it's her decision."*

In the end, when we could have gone either direction, we came back to this very scripture. It didn't matter what was *easier* or *justified* for us to do, it mattered what God had asked us to do in this child's life. In that context, the scrutiny was just a part of the process—learning tool that God used to sharpen, teach and equip us. The truth is, this isn't about us at all – it's about her. As we kept our eyes focused on what God's will was for this particular daughter's life, we were able to see clearly where we needed to soften our approach and where we needed to stand our ground.

As you go through the foster or adoption process, you'll face many questions in narrowing the type, age, and condition of the child you are willing to take into your home. Will you accept a child who has been sexually abused? Will you accept a child with physical or mental disabilities? Will you accept an older child? These are important considerations. Take time to thoroughly evaluate your capacity, ability, and life circumstances. Be real with yourself and with God. But don't be afraid to be honest about your fears. Be willing to lay them down and let God guide you according to His divine plan. Sometimes the things we fear most bring us the most opportunity for growth and joy.

Jesus was fully human and fully God. In that defining moment when he was alone in the Garden, he asked his Father a very human question, "If there's another way of doing this, please show me . . . . But, regardless of how I feel right now, not my will but yours be done." Are you willing to surrender your idea of how this process should go and give God total control?

Scripture Meditation: Take a few moments to read the following scriptures. Allow the Holy Spirit to speak to your heart about each of them.

Mark 14:35–36 (NLT) He went on a little farther and fell to the ground. He prayed that, if it were possible, the awful hour awaiting him might pass him by. "Abba, Father, he cried out, "everything is possible for you. Please take this cup of suffering away from me. Yet I want your will to be done, not mine"

Matthew 16:24 (NLT) Then Jesus said to his disciples, "If any of you wants to be my follower, you must turn from your selfish ways, take up your cross and follow me."

Philippians 2:5–8 (NLT) You must have the same attitude that Christ Jesus had. Though he was God, he did not think of equality with God as something to cling to. Instead, he gave up his divine privileges; he took the humble position of a slave and was born as a human being. When he appeared in human form, he humbled himself in obedience to God and died a criminal's death on a cross.

Capturing Thoughts: Throughout your adoption journey, I encourage you to capture your thoughts, fears, moments of joy, memories, and challenges. It will be a great encouragement to go back and read what you've written. You'll be surprised how much you and your family grow through your experiences.

Prayer Starter: Father, we have some real fears about this process. Our parenting has real limits. Help us to trust you with it all. We want your perfect plan to be at work in our family and all its future members. Please show us any area in our hearts that is being ruled by fear. Help us to lay that fear aside. We know that with you all things are possible and that you will never give us more than we can bear.

Discussion Questions – Day 3: Not My Will, But Yours Be Done

1. Talk about a time when your will was in conflict with God's will. What did you do? What influence did that experience have on your faith in God?

2. What is one thing you'll have to give up as a result of your involvement in foster care and adoption? Why is that sacrifice worth it to you?

3. Read Matthew 16:24. What are some ways that foster care or adoption will require you to take up your cross and follow Jesus?

4. What fears do you have about the foster care or adoption process? What is one thing you can do this week to help you put that fear aside and trust God's will?

My Journey:

(Use this space to capture your thoughts, prayers, concerns and questions)

SEARCH ME, O GOD, AND KNOW MY HEART;

TEST ME AND KNOW MY ANXIOUS THOUGHTS.

PSALM 139:23

DAY 4: SEARCH MY HEART

Going through the adoption and foster care process is all consuming. A pregnant woman thinks about her unborn child daily, wondering what he will look like and what kind of personality he will have. Adoptive and foster parents experience the same emotions and state of wonder. Although for the most part those emotions are positive, it's the hidden fears, anxiety, and worry in our hearts that will trip us up.

As a trainer for our state's foster care/adoption program, I often use an exercise called *The Dream Child*. The purpose of the exercise is to have the prospective parents draw a picture of their future foster or adopted child. What are their likes, dislikes, hobbies, etc.? Inevitably the families apply attributes to their future children that match their own. When my husband and I completed the exercise we were a one-child family whose favorite family activity was sitting at Barnes & Nobles reading for hours on end. It was important to us that our future child love reading, so we included books in our drawing. Fast-forward nine months to the placement of our new daughter, Heather. She hated reading—with a passion. That one seemingly small fact resulted in a major shift in our family's routine. It wasn't easy and it required us to leave our comfort zone and redefine a core part of our family so that our new daughter would feel at home.

The type of shift we made because our new daughter disliked reading isn't something that some families are willing to make. Heather vividly remembers another prospective parent coming for visits at her group home. She took her out to eat in order to get to know her with the intention of adoption. This particular woman was a librarian and when she discovered that Heather hated reading, she suddenly stopped showing up for visits. To this day, Heather can recount the moment that she revealed her dislike of reading. The librarian's entire demeanor changed and she quickly ended the visit. The librarian didn't want to parent *any* child, she wanted to parent a child whose likes/dislikes mirrored her own. If we were to ask her, she would probably say that she was afraid that she would have nothing in common with a child who didn't value reading. It was a terrible disappointment to Heather. But can you imagine what would have happened if the librarian had ignored her own worry and adopted Heather anyway, thinking she could change her? The end result could have been disastrous for both of them.

> **"It's important to let God search your heart and reveal the fears, anxieties and worries that might derail your journey or create tensions later on."**

It's important to let God search your heart and reveal the fears, anxieties, and worries that might derail your journey or create tensions later on. I've known men who were so afraid of being accused of sexual misconduct that they've completely withheld physical affection from their daughters, leaving the daughters feeling unloved and unwanted. I've known moms who let their own insecurities prevent them from addressing their children's behavior and give in to any demand. This led to teenagers who got into all kinds of trouble because they knew their mothers would never confront them. Giving in to our fears, insecurities, and worries may seem insignificant now, but the long-term effects on our children can be devastating.

Give God access to those hidden areas of your heart. Be honest with Him and with your spouse about your fears, insecurities, and worries. God is good. He already knows what's hidden in your heart. He's waiting for you to open up and give Him full access so He can bring healing and direction.

Scripture Meditation: Take a few moments to read the following scriptures. Allow the Holy Spirit to speak to your heart about each of them.

Psalm 139:1–18, 23 & 24 (NLT) O Lord, you have examined my heart and know everything about me. You know when I sit down or stand up. You know my thoughts even when I'm far away. You see me when I travel and when I rest at home. You know what I am going to say even before I say it, Lord. You go before me and follow me. You place your hand of blessing on my head. Such knowledge is too wonderful for me, too great for me to understand! I can never escape from your Spirit! I can never get away from your presence! If I go up to heaven, you are there; if I go down to the grave, you are there. If I ride the wings of the morning, if I dwell by the farthest oceans, even there your hand will guide me, and your strength will support me. I could ask the darkness to hide me and the light around me to become night – but even in darkness I cannot hide from you. To you the night shines as bright as day. Darkness and light are the same to you. You made all the delicate, inner parts of my body and knit me together in my mother's womb. Thank you for making me so wonderfully complex! Your workmanship is marvelous – how well I know it. You watched me as I was being formed in utter seclusion, as I was woven together in the dark of the womb. You saw me before I was born. Every day of my life was recorded in your book. Every moment was laid out before a single day had passed. How precious are your thoughts about me, O God. They cannot be numbered! I can't even count them; they outnumber the grains of sand! And when I wake up, you are still with me! Search me, O God, and know my heart; test me and know my anxious thoughts. Point out anything in me that offends you, and lead me along the path of everlasting life.

1 Samuel 16:7 (NLT) But the Lord said to Samuel, "Don't judge by his appearance or height, for I have rejected him. The Lord doesn't see things the way you see them. People judge by outward appearance, but the Lord looks at the heart.

1 Kings 8:39 (NLT) …then hear from heaven where you live, and forgive. Give your people what their actions deserve, for you alone know each human heart.

Capturing Thoughts: Throughout your adoption journey, I encourage you to capture your thoughts, fears, moments of joy, memories, and challenges. It will be a great encouragement to go back and read what you've written. You'll be surprised how much you and your family grow through your experiences.

Prayer Starter: Father, we invite you to search our hearts and expose any hidden fears that might hinder us from accomplishing your purposes in this journey. Teach us to be an open book before you, being honest about our thoughts and insecurities so that we can receive your healing and instruction.

Discussion Questions – Day 4: Search My Heart

1. Today's devotion says to give God access to those hidden areas of your heart. Be honest with Him and with your spouse about your fears, insecurities, and worries. How is that idea challenging? How is it liberating?

2. Respond to Heather's story. What thoughts and emotions did it stir in you?

3. Talk about the relationship between preparing yourself as much as possible for the challenges of fostering and trusting God to work through you in the lives of children despite the damage you've suffered in your life. How do you know when you need to hand something over to God?

4. What are some personal fears you need to hand over to God in prayer?

My Journey:

(Use this space to capture your thoughts, prayers, concerns and questions)

THE WHOLE POINT OF WHAT WE'RE URGING IS SIMPLY *LOVE*—LOVE

UNCONTAMINATED BY SELF-INTEREST AND COUNTERFEIT FAITH,

A LIFE OPEN TO GOD.

I TIMOTHY 1:5

DAY 5: PURE MOTIVES

Adoption is popular. It's become one of the "it" topics in church, at church conferences, and among our peer groups. Even celebrities are doing it. In many circles, adopted children have become a cute accessory to carry around, post pictures of on social media and answer questions about in order to appear selfless and draw in the admiration of others. Adopting children of a different race is especially adorable.

You may want to dismiss everything I wrote in the preceding paragraph as cruel, but let's face it: in America, adoption is currently *en vogue*. When adoption becomes fashionable, children suffer. Equally important, parents suffer. The idea of living like the Joneses may sound appealing, but the reality of adoption is anything but glamorous. Digging into the reasons—the *real* reasons—you want to adopt is critical. You should ask yourself the crucial questions about your motives, look deep inside, and accept the honest answers. Only then will God begin to minister to your heart.

Even in foster care, which isn't nearly as popular as adoption, our motives must be evaluated. Foster parents, by necessity, live a different kind of life. Birth parent visits, court visits, countless forms, social workers, CASA

31

volunteers and more. To be a foster parent requires you to lay aside the idea of normal in your family and routine. If your motives aren't carefully examined; your journey will be extremely difficult. There are many reasons that people enter foster care – to provide a temporary place of healing for a hurting child, to supplement their finances, to work with families in crisis or as an entry point to adoption. Regardless of the motive for entering foster care or adoption, it's imperative that you examine your decision carefully.

> **"Regardless of the motive for entering foster care or adoption, it's imperative that you examine your decision carefully."**

Whether it's a "rescue the children" reason, an "add to our family" reason, a "look at how good I am" reason, or a genuine call of God to bind up wounds and provide restoration, only you and God can decide. Each of us has a motive for pursuing foster care and adoption. For my husband and me, our initial motivator was adding to our family. It's our responsibility as believers to guard our hearts against selfish ambitions or vain conceit.

Unexamined motives set us up for failure. Unvoiced expectations come back to haunt us as disappointment, frustration and discouragement. Many times the core of our discontent can be traced back to an unmet expectation that we had when we entered the process. But if your motives are like those described in 1 Timothy 1:5—to open yourself to God and love, uncontaminated by self-interest or counterfeit faith—you'll have no expectation but to see Jesus Christ glorified through your efforts and trials. This gives you the freedom to really love and the ability to release any guilt or frustration in difficult moments.

Whatever your motive, I want to make one thing clear: caring for children who've experienced abuse, rejection and trauma is hard. This is really, really hard work. But you aren't alone.

Scripture Meditation: Take a few moments to read the following scriptures. Allow the Holy Spirit to speak to your heart about each of them.

> **Proverbs 21:2** (NLT) People may be right in their own eyes, but the Lord examines their heart.

> **Matthew 6:1** (NLT) Watch out! Don't do your good deeds publicly, to be admired by others, for you will lose the reward from your Father in heaven.

> **1 Samuel 16:7** (NLT) But the Lord said to Samuel, "Don't judge by his appearance or height, for I have rejected him. The Lord doesn't see things the way you see them. People judge by outward appearance, but the Lord looks at the heart."

Capturing Thoughts: Throughout your adoption journey, I encourage you to capture your thoughts, fears, moments of joy, memories, and challenges. It will be a great encouragement to go back and read what you've written. You'll be surprised how much you and your family grow through your experiences.

Prayer Starter: Lord, examine our hearts and let your Word be a mirror into our souls. We want to walk in your footsteps, care for your children, love the unloved, and accept the unaccepted. Reveal any areas of our hearts that are corrupted by selfishness or vain conceit. Open our eyes to see the truth. Speak to us about your will for our journey.

Discussion Questions – Day 5: Pure Motives

1. What are your reasons for entering foster care or adoption? How was God involved in your decision?

2. Today's devotion says, "To be a foster parent requires you to lay aside the idea of normal in your family and routine; if your motives aren't carefully examined, your journey will be extremely difficult." Respond to that statement. Do you agree? Why or why not?

3. 1 Timothy 1:5 talks about love contaminated by self-interest. What are some ways that fostering or adopting can be contaminated by self-interest? How can you protect your heart from them?

4. If unexamined motives set us up for failure, what is one thing you can do this week to examine or re-examine your motives for getting involved in foster care or adoption? What can this group do to support you or hold you accountable?

My Journey:

(Use this space to capture your thoughts, prayers, concerns and questions)

DAY 6: WISDOM

In this journey, you need wisdom more than anything—more than a compassionate heart, a spirit of resolve, or a profound dream. The dictionary definition of wisdom is "the quality of having experience, knowledge, and good judgment." More than likely, you've never parented a wounded child before so you don't have the experience or knowledge to confidently make good judgments in the process. This is where seeking outside wisdom comes in.

During a period of great difficulty with one of our daughters, I vividly remember her counselor saying to me, "Based on everything I've seen and heard, she's a classic case of RAD (Reactive Attachment Disorder)." Although the phrase scared me, I wasn't completely caught off guard because I had already invested time learning about attachment disorders in foster and adopted children. Although having head-knowledge about an issue and dealing with it personally are totally different, I had a head start on understanding our journey as a family because I understood the basics of the issue. This basic understanding helped me begin to connect with the brokenness that she felt inside instead of blaming her for the outward behaviors that made it difficult to parent her.

There's a saying: "knowledge is power." It definitely applies to trauma-

36

centered parenting. Too often, potential parents enter the adoption process with little knowledge of the challenges they may face, including birth family connections, emotional issues, or strange behaviors. When face-to-face with a child dealing with one or more of these issues, adoptive parents get trapped in fear. They wonder what they've gotten themselves into and feel ill equipped to continue the journey.

> **"Too often, potential parents enter the adoption process with little knowledge of the challenges they may face, including birth family connections, emotional issues or strange behaviors."**

Knowledge truly is power. If you spend time before your placement learning about common disorders and how others have successfully dealt with them, you'll feel more at ease when facing similar issues in your child. When your child bursts out in anger or you find a mountain of food hidden in his room, you won't panic. Instead, you'll rely on the knowledge and wisdom you've gained. You will be equipped to handle the situation with confidence and calm.

When we ask God for wisdom in a specific area, our eyes can be opened to resources, individuals, and opportunities to learn and grow.

Scripture Meditation: Take a few moments to read the following scriptures. Allow the Holy Spirit to speak to your heart about each of them.

Proverbs 21:2 (NLT) People may be right in their own eyes, but the

Lord examines their heart.

Proverbs 3:14-23 (NLT) For wisdom is more profitable than silver, and her wages are better than gold. Wisdom is more precious than rubies; nothing you desire can compare with her. She offers you long life in her right hand, and riches and honor in her left. She will guide you down delightful paths; all her ways are satisfying. Wisdom is a tree of life to those who embrace her; happy are those who hold her tightly. By wisdom the Lord founded the earth; by understanding he created the heavens. By his knowledge the deep fountains of the earth burst forth, and the dew settles beneath the night sky. My child, don't lose sight of common sense and discernment. Hang on to them, for they will refresh your soul. They are like jewels on a necklace. They keep you safe on your way and your feet will not stumble.

Proverbs 4:7 (NLT) Getting wisdom is the wisest thing you can do! And whatever else you do, develop good judgment.

Proverbs 15:22 (NLT) Plans go wrong for lack of advice; many advisers bring success.

Capturing Thoughts: Throughout your adoption journey, I encourage you to capture your thoughts, fears, moments of joy, memories, and challenges. It will be a great encouragement to go back and read what you've written. You'll be surprised how much you and your family grow through your experiences.

Prayer Starter: Lord, we ask you for wisdom about parenting wounded children. We ask for understanding to prepare us for the journey ahead. Lead us to the right people, open doors to the right conversations, and guide us to resources that will provide the knowledge to strengthen us in our journey.

Discussion Questions – Day 6: Wisdom

1. Talk about a person in your life whose behavior frustrates you. What approach do you take to deal with that frustration?

2. Today's devotion says, "Knowledge truly is power. If you spend time before your placement learning about common disorders and how others have successfully dealt with them, you'll feel more at ease when facing similar issues in your child." How does having knowledge result in wisdom in dealing with foster and adopted children? What role does application play in gaining wisdom?

3. Read Proverbs 15:22. Talk about the benefits of having many advisors.

4. Who are some people that can give you wise counsel regarding foster care or adoption? What is one thing you can do this week to begin to engage those people? What can this group do to help you?

My Journey:

(Use this space to capture your thoughts, prayers, concerns and questions)

By faith Abraham, when called to go to a place he would later receive as his inheritance, obeyed and went, even though he did not know where he was going.

HEBREWS 11:8

DAY 7: OBEDIENCE

"I'm absolutely certain that this is what God has asked me to do." It's that same certainty that Abraham must have felt when God asked him in Genesis 12:1–4 to leave everything behind and go to a place that He would show him. Because Abraham was absolutely certain that he had heard God's voice, he packed up and left—without a Google map, without a written plan, without a destination. He just went. He had no idea how long the journey would be or where he would end up. He just knew that God had spoken and there was only one appropriate response to His voice: obedience.

"As you hear the call of the Father to open your life and home to the fatherless, you will be required to step forward in obedience."

As you hear the call of the Father to open your life and home to the fatherless, you will be required to step forward in obedience. Your journey may feel a lot like Abraham's. God won't give you a roadmap. He won't send you a detailed timeline of events. He'll ask you to trust Him with the destination. The only thing He'll give you is *hope in your heart*. The good news is that's all you need.

In the middle of this journey, you'll experience times of uncertainty. It might take longer than you hoped. You might have a country, an age or a gender in mind only to discover that's not the destination He has in mind. There may be important people in your life who disagree with your decision. Just like Abraham, your obedience to God's call can't be based on your own ideas of where you are going, or others' opinions of what you should do. Can you still obey?

Another consideration in God's call to foster or adopt is how you're going to handle the tough times. We've all heard the phrase, "When the going gets tough, the tough get going." With certainty, the one thing you can count on in this journey is this: the going *will* get tough. So what does the latter part of that phrase mean to you, "…the tough get going…?" Does it mean quit and run, or buckle down and persist? Children coming into your care permanently or temporarily who've been abused, neglected and abandoned require a lot of patience and commitment. There *will* be days where quitting will seem like the best option for you and for the child. It's on those days that you have to be absolutely certain that God has called you to this place. He can lead you to resources, counsel, and direction, but only as you fully obey His call.

Obedience to this call draws you into uncharted territories. In uncharted places, we can find ourselves weary and afraid. In the midst of our discomfort, fear, and uncertainty is a simple word: faith. Faith and obedience are partners. Together, they are the fuel for pursuing God's call on our lives. Are you ready to travel?

◆◆◆

Scripture Meditation: Take a few moments to read the following scriptures. Allow the Holy Spirit to speak to your heart about each of them.

Genesis 12:1–4 (NLT) The Lord had said to Abram, "Leave your native country, your relatives, and your father's family, and go to the land that I will show you. I will make you into a great nation. I will bless you and make you famous, and you will be a blessing to others. I will bless those who bless you and curse those who treat you with contempt. All the families on earth will be blessed through you." So Abram departed as the Lord had instructed, and Lot went with him. Abram was seventy-five years old when he left Haran.

1 Samuel 15:22 (NLT) But Samuel replied, "What is more pleasing to the Lord: your burnt offerings and sacrifices or your obedience to his voice? Listen! Obedience is better than sacrifice, and submission is better than offering the fat of rams."

James 1:22 (NLT) But don't just listen to God's word. You must do what it says. Otherwise, you are only fooling yourselves.

Isaiah 1:19 (NLT) If you will only obey me, you will have plenty to eat.

2 Corinthians 2:9 (NLT) I wrote to you as I did to test you and see if you would fully comply with my instructions.

Capturing Thoughts: Throughout your adoption journey, I encourage you to capture your thoughts, fears, and moments of joy, memories, and challenges. It will be a great encouragement to go back and read what you've written. You'll be surprised how much you and your family grow through your experiences.

Prayer Starter: Father, thank you for the hope that you've placed in our hearts. We commit to trust you in the journey and walk in faith, as Abraham, understanding that as we follow you, we may discover our destination is not what we expected. We know that your plans for us are better than anything we could imagine ourselves.

Discussion Questions – Day 7: Obedience

1. Talk about a time when obedience to God caused you discomfort. What happened?

2. Today's devotion says, "There *will* be days where quitting will seem like the best option for you and for the child." In what ways does that idea challenge you?

3. Has anyone in your life had a negative reaction to your desire to be involved in foster care or adoption? How did that affect your desire?

4. What is one thing that scares you about foster care or adoption? How has it influenced your obedience to God's call?

My Journey:

(Use this space to capture your thoughts, prayers, concerns and questions)

RELIGION THAT GOD OUR FATHER ACCEPTS AS PURE AND FAULTLESS IS THIS:

TO LOOK AFTER ORPHANS AND WIDOWS IN THEIR DISTRESS AND TO KEEP

ONESELF FROM BEING POLLUTED BY THE WORLD.

JAMES 1:27

DAY 8: PURE AND FAULTLESS RELIGION

When we think of "religion," images of prayer, Bible reading, preaching, and evangelizing naturally surface. Each of these things has an important place in our walk with Jesus, but James 1:27 points out that pure and faultless religion is to look after orphans and widows in their distress. What does that really mean? James points us to a kind of religion that is radically selfless and concerned with the most vulnerable around us. If we're not careful, religion can be self-serving. We can study the Bible and pray to find out how to get the most out of God for ourselves. We can preach and evangelize for personal gain or to puff up our egos. Even as we step forward in faith to obey the call of James 1:27, we must continue to evaluate our own motives and guard our hearts against selfishness. It's more difficult to be selfish while trying to meet the physical, emotional, and spiritual needs of others – but it's not impossible.

I remember talking to God in a moment of complete exhaustion after a week of really late nights dealing with one of my daughters' behaviors. In complete weariness I said, "Lord, I just don't know why I'm having to deal with this. It shouldn't be this hard. I'm exhausted, I need sleep and I still have to work tomorrow." Almost immediately, I felt a statement rise in my spirit, "You wouldn't be so exhausted if you spent less emotional energy feeling sorry for yourself and how much this is costing you." Ouch. The truth in that moment was this: I had spent every night that week struggling not only with the behavior, but also (more importantly) with the fact that the behavior was impacting me—my time, my attention and my routine. Romans 15:1 & 2 instructs us in this way, *"We who are strong ought to bear with the failings of the weak and not to please ourselves. Each of us should please his neighbor for his good, to build him up."* Once again, I found myself reminded of my own heart's ability for selfishness. As foster and adoptive parents, the children that God brings into our care need us to bear with them, especially in their failings, because they are weak. We are strong and it's our job to continually remind ourselves that this journey isn't about us.

"As foster and adoptive parents, the children that God brings into our care need us to bear with them, especially in their failings, because they are weak."

It's not easy to practice the kind of religion that calls you to lay down your life for others. But that's the call of the cross. The cross wasn't comfortable. Jesus was exhausted from a week of struggle by the time He was nailed there—for us. As imitators of Jesus, we are instructed to give our all on behalf of those less fortunate.

Pure and faultless religion requires us to lay down our dreams of comfort in order to pick up another's brokenness, anger, pain, loneliness, bitterness, and resentment. Bearing that burden with them may cost us time, money, and friends, but we can be confident that God sees a reflection of His Son in us, His pure and faultless Son.

Scripture Meditation: Take a few moments to read the following scriptures. Allow the Holy Spirit to speak to your heart about each of them.

1 Samuel 2:8 (NLT) He lifts the poor from the dust and the needy from the garbage dump. He sets them among princes, placing them in seats of honor. For all of the earth is the Lord's, and he has set the world in order.

Proverbs 19:17 (NLT) If you help the poor, you are lending to the Lord – and he will repay you.

Proverbs 14:31 (NLT) Those who oppress the poor insult their Maker, but helping the poor honors him.

Psalm 82:3 (NLT) Give justice to the poor and the orphan; uphold the rights of the oppressed and the destitute.

Proverbs 21:3 (NLT) The Lord is more pleased when we do what is right and just than when we offer sacrifices to him.

Capturing Thoughts: Throughout your adoption journey, I encourage you to capture your thoughts, fears, and moments of joy, memories, and challenges. It will be a great encouragement to go back and read what you've written. You'll be surprised how much you and your family grow through your experiences.

Prayer Starter: Lord, test our hearts for selfish ambition so we can pursue this journey with purity and faultlessness. Show us your heart for the hurting, the desolate, and the fatherless. Burn it deep within our spirits so that we see with eyes of faith and compassion.

Discussion Questions – Day 8: Pure and Faultless Religion

1. Do you think most people consider the word "religion" warm and personal or cold and institutional? How do the words of James 1:27 challenge our cultural assumptions about religion?

2. Talk about a time that you left your comfort zone to do something for someone else. How did your effort impact the relationship?

3. Read James 1:27 again. How does it apply to foster children since they're not legally orphans?

4. What is the biggest sacrifice you've made for someone else? What did it cost you? Do you regret it?

My Journey:

(Use this space to capture your thoughts, prayers, concerns and questions)

BUT YOU, GOD, SEE THE TROUBLE OF THE AFFLICTED; YOU CONSIDER THEIR

GRIEF AND TAKE IT IN HAND. THE VICTIMS COMMIT THEMSELVES TO YOU;

YOU ARE THE HELPER OF THE FATHERLESS.

PSALM 10:14

DAY 9: THE FATHERLESS

In spiritual terms, being fatherless means being without covering, security, or direction. It means wandering alone in the world without a guide. It means being lost. The Aramaic word translated "orphan" or "fatherless" originally meant, "to be lonely or bereaved." It is used over forty times in the Old Testament. Can you imagine having no identity—no one who claims you, loves you, provides for you, or leaves a legacy for you to follow?

> **"Can you imagine having no identity—no one who claims you, loves you, provides for you, or leaves a legacy for you to follow?"**

Before we met Jesus, all of us were without hope and a future. Yet, God reached down and brought us into His family. He calls us sons and daughters and gives us His very identity. Everything that He has is ours. We have an inheritance, a future, and hope. When I truly stop to think about all that Jesus did for me so that I could become an adopted daughter of God, I'm speechless.

As imitators of Christ, we offer the same to the lonely, the bereaved, the *fatherless*. Scripture is clear about our duty to care for the fatherless. God's eye is on them. His mighty hand of justice is against anyone who takes advantage of or oppresses them. We are to care for them, visit them, and allow them to share in the blessings of our lives. Caring and providing for the fatherless is an inescapable command for followers of Jesus Christ.

When I consider all that my children have lost, I am overwhelmed with gratitude that God chose me to parent and love them. To be trusted to care for someone so precious to Him is an immense honor. One of my favorite verses is Psalm 68:5-6, *"God is a father to the fatherless... He places the lonely in families..."* For each of our daughters, God saw their loneliness and He *placed* them in our family. There are times that I find myself overwhelmed as I watch them celebrate a special moment and realize how lucky I am to be there to share it with them. I never want to betray that trust or be another adult to abandon or shame them.

Just as Jesus poured Himself out on the cross to make us co-heirs with Him, it is our call as Christians to pour ourselves out for the orphan. I love this quote from John Piper: "Many things in this life are utterly opposite from the way they seem. And here is one of them. When the children of God— the followers of Jesus—are permitted to suffer in the path of love, the path of orphan care, God is giving a gift to the world."

You are a gift to the world. This journey that you're on, through pitfall and pain, is the call of Christ for the fatherless.

Scripture Meditation: Take a few moments to read the following scriptures. Allow the Holy Spirit to speak to your heart about each of them.

Exodus 22:22–24 (NLT) You must not exploit a widow or an orphan. If you exploit them in any way and they cry out to me, then I will certainly hear their cry. My anger will blaze against you, and I will kill you with the sword. Then your wives will be widows and your children fatherless.

Deuteronomy 10:18 (NLT) He ensures that orphans and widows receive justice. He shows love to the foreigners living among you and gives them food and clothing.

Deuteronomy 26:12–13 (NLT) Every third year you must offer a special tithe of your crops. In this year of the special tithe you must give your tithe to the Levites, foreigners, orphans, and widows, so that they will have enough to eat in your towns. Then you must declare in the presence of the Lord your God, "I have taken the sacred gift from my house and given it to the Levites, foreigners, orphans, and widows, just as you commanded me. I have not violated or forgotten any of your commands.

Psalm 68:5–6 (NLT) Father to the fatherless, defender of widows – this is God, whose dwelling is holy. God places the lonely in families; he sets the prisoners free and gives them joy. But he makes the rebellious live in a sun-scorched land.

Psalm 82:3–4 (NLT) Give justice to the poor and the orphan; uphold the rights of the oppressed and the destitute. Rescue the poor and helpless; deliver them from the grasp of evil people.

Capturing Thoughts: Throughout your adoption journey, I encourage you to capture your thoughts, fears, moments of joy, memories, and challenges. It will be a great encouragement to go back and read what you've written. You'll be surprised how much you and your family grow through your experiences.

Prayer Starter: Father, thank you for caring for us and loving us, for giving us an inheritance in Christ Jesus, and for calling us your own. Show us how you would have us use our lives so that we can give your precious children a place to belong, somewhere to call home.

Discussion Questions—Day 9: The Fatherless

1. Have you imagined what the first day with your first foster or adopted child will be like? If so, what did you imagine?

2. Read Exodus 22:22-24. Why do you think God holds a special place in his heart for widows and orphans?

3. In today's devotion, being fatherless is described as, "…being without covering, security, or direction. It means wandering alone in the world without a guide." What emotions does that stir in you?

4. What scares or worries you about the idea of putting the needs of a foster or adopted child ahead of your own?

My Journey:

(Use this space to capture your thoughts, prayers, concerns and questions)

SING, BARREN WOMAN, WHO HAS NEVER HAD A BABY.

FILL THE AIR WITH SONG, YOU WHO'VE NEVER EXPERIENCED CHILDBIRTH!

YOU'RE ENDING UP WITH FAR MORE CHILDREN THAN ALL THOSE CHILDBEARING

WOMEN. "GOD SAYS SO!" CLEAR LOTS OF GROUND FOR YOUR TENTS! MAKE

YOUR TENTS LARGE. SPREAD OUT! THINK BIG! USE PLENTY OF ROPE, DRIVE THE

TENT PEGS DEEP. YOU'RE GOING TO NEED LOTS OF ELBOW ROOM FOR YOUR

GROWING FAMILY. YOU'RE GOING TO TAKE OVER WHOLE NATIONS; YOU'RE

GOING TO RESETTLE ABANDONED CITIES. DON'T BE AFRAID—YOU'RE NOT

GOING TO BE EMBARRASSED. DON'T HOLD BACK—YOU'RE NOT GOING TO COME

UP SHORT.

ISAIAH 54:2 (MSG)

DAY 10: ENLARGE YOUR TENT

Isaiah tells us to sing, even in childlessness, because God has a plan to expand our families. So get ready! And, make sure you have plenty of room!

That sounds really exciting, right? In the early stages of considering foster care and adoption, it's the center of our greatest hope. We want to add children to our empty rooms. We can't wait to celebrate holidays, go on vacations and walk into a restaurant and say, "Party of ____!"

As you prepare for the moment of placement, have you considered the other ways in which your family might grow? Many foster and adoptive parents find themselves enlarging their tents by also enlarging their hearts to accept their child's birth-family connections.

Have you thought about interacting with the child's birth mom? Dad? Sister? Brother? Have you considered expanding your heart to genuinely love and care for them, regardless of the circumstances that led to their child becoming your child?

> **"...the idea of even having a conversation with a parent who had abused and neglected their child was not appealing to us."**

When my husband and I first went through the training and approval process for our state, the idea of even having a conversation with a parent who had abused and neglected their child was not appealing to us. We were supposed to protect our future kids from the people who had hurt them. Why on earth would we seek them out?

What we didn't consider was that these family members, regardless of the situation, were a vital part of each of our children's identities. By accepting our children's natural connection to their birth families, we also fully accept our children. There is tremendous healing power in children knowing that you're willing to love every part of who they are and where they came from.

Since those initial reservations, we've embraced birth family connections with all of our children. Some have really close relationships with their birth parents, some don't. That's okay. We're willing to explore the relationship based on where the individual child is at and where their birth family is at, letting wisdom and love guide us. The results have been miraculous in terms of healing for our children and their birth families. It hasn't always been easy, comfortable, or fun, but it's been worth it. We've found an open door to a part of our children's hearts that may have otherwise been locked away forever.

As you enter the process of adoption, prepare your heart to include those beyond the children you bring into your family. Like me, you may be surprised to find that you enjoy larger tents.

Scripture Meditation: Take a few moments to read the following scriptures. Allow the Holy Spirit to speak to your heart about each of them.

> **2 Corinthians 9:10** (NLT) For God is the one who provides seed for the farmer and then bread to eat. In the same way, he will provide and increase your resources and then produce a great harvest of generosity in you.

> **Psalm 119:32** (NLT) I will pursue your commands for you expand my understanding.

> **Deuteronomy 1:11** (NLT) And may the Lord, the God of your ancestors, multiply you a thousand times more and bless you as he promised.

Capturing Thoughts: Throughout your adoption journey, I encourage you to capture your thoughts, fears, moments of joy, memories, and challenges. It will be a great encouragement to go back and read what you've written. You'll be surprised how much you and your family grow through your experiences.

Prayer Starter: Lord, stretch our hearts to include anyone you would have us love in this journey. Give us the grace to get beyond our reservations, disgust, anger, stereotypes, and prejudices to love as you love, for the sake of your precious children.

Discussion Questions – Day 10: Enlarge Your Tent

1. Think about a person that offered you encouragement during a crucial time in your life. What did that encouragement do for you?

2. Read Psalm 119:32. What does it mean to pursue God's commands? What is the relationship between pursuing His commands and gaining understanding or wisdom?

3. When has God given you the opportunity to encourage someone who was different from you in some way? How did that experience change your perspective on God?

4. Talk about a time when you had to win someone's trust. What did you do? If you could do it all again, would you do anything differently?

My Journey:

(Use this space to capture your thoughts, prayers, concerns and questions)

MOSES SPOKE TO THE HEADS OF THE TRIBES OF THE PEOPLE OF ISRAEL,

SAYING, "THIS IS WHAT THE LORD HAS COMMANDED. IF A MAN VOWS A VOW

TO THE LORD, OR SWEARS AN OATH TO BIND HIMSELF BY A PLEDGE, HE SHALL

NOT BREAK HIS WORD. HE SHALL DO ACCORDING TO ALL THAT PROCEEDS OUT

OF HIS MOUTH."

NUMBERS 30:1 & 2

DAY 11: 'TIL DEATH DO US PART

Adoption is legal and permanent. It's an *in sickness and in health, 'til death do us part* covenant. The moment you enter a child's life and commit with your words to be their *forever family*, you enter a covenant before God. The legal proceedings simply put on paper what God has already ordained in heaven. Both the natural legal process and the spiritual covenant are binding *for life*.

Just as our spiritual adoption into the Kingdom of God indicates a permanent relationship with God as our heavenly Father, natural adoption is a permanent relationship in which we promise a lifetime of belonging in our families, no matter what.

Foster care is also a commitment. It's a commitment to covenant relationship. When a child is placed in your home, you've committed to protect them, love them, and provide for them until the time comes for them to return to their family or enter permanency in another way. This type of covenant is also binding before God, until the time comes for its natural end.

Just as God, through Jesus, became flesh and walked with us temporarily on this earth, we are to be His temporary hands and feet in the lives of foster children who enter our care. Our commitment as foster parents is to affirm, lead and guide each child for as long as God allows, even when it's hard.

In both adoption and foster care, it's the *even when it's hard/ no matter what* part that often trips parents up. Trust me, things can get hard with your adopted and foster children . . . *really hard*. Things can also get really hard with your biological children. The difference is, there's no way to send your biological children back when their behavior has pushed you to your absolute limits. When they misbehave, there's no choice but to work through the issue and continue forward.

In training, I often caution parents not to treat the foster care and adoption process like shopping for a used car. Kids are not meant to be "tried out" and "sent back" if they don't meet your needs. This process isn't about finding the right child to meet your needs; it's about being the right parent to meet theirs.

> **"This process isn't about finding the right child to meet your needs; it's about being the right parent to meet theirs."**

Foster and adoptive parents must take on a mindset of perseverance. Your children are your children—no matter what—whether by birth or by choice. Regardless of how extreme their behavior, remember that you're in a covenant. You committed, *for better or for worse*. When you honor covenant, God honors you. He will give you the strength, wisdom, and understanding to turn the situation around for good.

Scripture Meditation: Take a few moments to read the following scriptures. Allow the Holy Spirit to speak to your heart about each of them.

Psalm 37:5 (NLT) Commit everything you do to the Lord. Trust him, and he will help you.

Proverbs 16:3 (NLT) Commit your actions to the Lord, and your plans will succeed.

Hebrews 4:14–16 (NLT) So then, since we have a great High Priest who has entered heaven, Jesus the Son of God, let us hold firmly to what we believe. This High Priest of ours understands our weaknesses, for he faced all of the same testing we do, yet he did not sin. So let us come boldly to the throne of our gracious God. There we will receive his mercy, and we will find grace to help us when we need it most.

Matthew 5:33–37 (NKJV) Again you have heard that it was said to those of old, 'You shall not swear falsely, but shall perform your oaths to the Lord.' But I say to you, do not swear at all: neither by heaven, for it's God's throne; nor by the earth, for it is His footstool; nor by Jerusalem, for it is the city of the great King. Nor shall you swear by your head, because you cannot make one hair white or black. But let your 'Yes' be 'Yes' and your 'No' be 'No.' For whatever is more than these is from the evil one.

Psalm 15:1–4 (NLT) Who may worship in your sanctuary, Lord? Who may enter your presence on your holy hill? Those who lead blameless lives and do what is right, speaking the truth from sincere hearts. Those who refuse to gossip or harm their neighbors or speak evil of their friends. Those who despise flagrant sinners, and honor the faithful followers of the Lord, and keep their promises even when it hurts.

Capturing Thoughts: Throughout your adoption journey, I encourage you to capture your thoughts, fears, moments of joy, memories, and challenges. It will be a great encouragement to go back and read what you've written. You'll be surprised how much you and your family grow through your experiences.

Prayer Starter: Father, as we travel this journey toward the placement of our child or children, help us to understand your covenant promise to us as your adopted sons and daughters. Help us love the children you bring into our families unconditionally. Thank you for your unconditional love and goodness toward us.

Discussion Questions – Day 11: 'Til Death Do Us Part

1. Talk about a time when you've broken off a difficult relationship. If you could go back in time, would you do things differently? Why or why not?

2. Have you thought and prayed about the fact that adoption is a lifetime commitment and a covenant before God, like marriage? Have you thought and prayed about foster care being a covenant relationship before God? Talk about how you feel God is dealing with your heart in this area.

3. Have you thought and prayed about what behaviors you are and are not willing to accept before saying yes to a foster child placement? Talk about the process you've gone through or are going through in order to answer these questions.

4. Today's devotion says, "Kids are not meant to be "tried out" and "sent back" if they don't meet your needs. This process isn't about finding the right child to meet your needs; it's about being the right parent to meet theirs." Respond to that statement. What emotions does it stir in you?

My Journey:

(Use this space to capture your thoughts, prayers, concerns and questions)

FOR THE SAKE OF CHRIST, THEN, I AM CONTENT WITH WEAKNESSES,

INSULTS, HARDSHIPS, PERSECUTIONS, AND CALAMITIES.

FOR WHEN I AM WEAK, THEN I AM STRONG.

2 CORINTHIANS 12:10

DAY 12: CONTENTMENT

In the face of difficulties that will inevitably arise, it's important to understand where a true sense of contentment comes from: Jesus Christ. Contentment doesn't mean that you're just satisfied with what you have or how things are and that you don't want change. Contentment is understanding what God has called you to do and trusting Him even in tough circumstances.

When your friends are worried about their teenagers dating or finding the right friends and you're staring out your door as the police pull in for the third time in a month to deal with yet another incidence of your teen's shenanigans, how do you handle the frustration? When all of the toddlers in your child's class seem sweet, cuddly, and adorable while your little one hits, punches, and bites, how can you avoid feeling embarrassed? It's natural to wonder if you made the wrong decision and covet a "normal" family experience. But it's important to remind yourself that God is in charge. He has a plan even when it doesn't feel "normal."

I recently heard Elizabeth Styffe from Saddleback Church say, "Remember, 'normal' is only a setting on the washing machine." That statement resonated within me because it was one of my biggest struggles early on. I still find it rearing its ugly head from time to time when our family dynamic gets into the tough places and I begin wondering if things are ever going to "get back to normal."

When we started this process, I mistakenly thought that we were going to add a child to our family and they were going to *love it*. The idea that the child would jump right into our routines, our hobbies, our way of life and that we'd all live happily ever after made perfect since to me. I didn't realize everything was about to completely change; even our family date nights.

Our first daughter from foster care hated everything that we enjoyed as a family. Reading was boring. Going camping was boring. Our food was boring. After coming to the realization that *we* were just boring, we had a choice to make. We could either be *her family* or force her to be *our child*. There's a distinction. We could either try to force her to change and like the things that we liked (endure them as we enjoyed them), or we could change to find other 'normals' that she liked. When I look back now, I agree with her. We were boring. Through her we learned to have more outward fun— playing family board games with lots of laughter and just being more active and social. Our 'normal' changed and it was okay. Every child that has entered our family since has resulted in a change of normal. We are not the family we used to be; we're better. We're more resilient and we adapt more easily.

Admittedly, some changes are easier than others. From time to time, our family normal has included violent outbursts (some of them mine), dealing with pornography on computers, visits from the police, running away, shoplifting, sexual exploration, teen pregnancy, residential treatment facilities, being called *lots* of creative things, stealing, food hoarding, suicide attempts and more. A friend once asked me how our family was doing and I responded, "Oh, it's just the Parish family normal." He laughed because he knew exactly what I meant: "If I tell you everything we've dealt with, this week alone, you'll think we're crazy."

> **"It's easy to get caught up in comparisons of what everyone else considers 'normal' child-rearing. But you have to remember that your experience is unique."**

It's easy to get caught up in comparisons of what everyone else considers "normal" child-rearing. But you have to remember that your experience is unique. Your calling is unique. Your children are unique. If you can remain in a place of trust, knowing what God has called you to do and staying committed to doing it, you'll find contentment regardless of your circumstances.

Your main priorities are God, your spouse, and your children—in that order. What others think or say is not your concern. Being content is this— knowing that you are exactly where you're suppose to be, even when it hurts.

Scripture Meditation: Take a few moments to read the following scriptures. Allow the Holy Spirit to speak to your heart about each of them.

Psalm 37:3–5 (NLT) Trust in the Lord and do good. Then you will live safely in the land and prosper. Take delight in the Lord, and he will give you your heart's desires. Commit everything you do to the Lord. Trust him, and he will help you.

Psalm 16:11 (NLT) You will show me the way of life, granting me the joy of your presence and the pleasures of living with you forever.

Psalm 55:22 (NLT) Give your burdens to the Lord, and he will take care of you. He will not permit the godly to slip and fall.

Proverbs 17:22 (NLT) A cheerful heart is good medicine, but a broken spirit saps a person's strength.

Philippians 3:7–8 (NLT) I once thought these things were valuable, but now I consider them worthless because of what Christ has done. Yes, everything else is worthless when compared with the infinite value of knowing Christ Jesus my Lord. For his sake I have discarded everything else, counting it all as garbage, so that I could gain Christ.

Capturing Thoughts: Throughout your adoption journey, I encourage you to capture your thoughts, fears, moments of joy, memories, and challenges. It will be a great encouragement to go back and read what you've written. You'll be surprised how much you and your family grow through your experiences.

Prayer Starter: Father, thank you for the calling you've placed on our hearts. As we walk this path with you, help us grow in wisdom so we're confident in this thing you've called us to do. We trust you to lead us and guide us in all things and give us a spirit of gratitude and satisfaction in you.

Discussion Questions – Day 12: Contentment

1. Describe the last time you were embarrassed by a child's behavior in public.

2. Talk about a time you were rejected because you were doing something that made others uncomfortable. What did you do?

3. What have you done to prepare for the possibility that family or friends may distance themselves from you because of your choice to take in children with histories of abuse? What, if anything, can this group do to help or support you?

4. Read Psalm 16:11. In what practical ways do you seek joy in God's presence?

My Journey:

(Use this space to capture your thoughts, prayers, concerns and questions)

THE PEACE OF GOD, WHICH SURPASSES ALL COMPREHENSION WILL GUARD
YOUR HEARTS AND YOUR MINDS IN CHRIST JESUS.

PHILIPPIANS 4:7

DAY 13: THE GIFT OF PEACE

We assume that having peace means having a stress-free life. But that's not what Scripture means when it tells us that God will grant us peace that "surpasses all comprehension." True peace is grounded in Christ. It's knowing beyond a shadow of a doubt that He is able to give you the strength and wisdom to overcome even the greatest difficulties.

The true peace of God is a shield around your heart and mind. It gives you the ability to see beyond your circumstances to a future grounded in Him. A runaway child, a trip to the emergency room for an overdose, a difficulty with birth parents, a tantrum that lasts for hours, or terrible news from your caseworker—each of these things can either steal your peace or strengthen your resolve. You alone decide.

Learning to accept the gift of peace that God offers isn't the same as living in denial. It's acknowledging that we live in a broken world full of broken people. Foster and adoptive parents feel the weight of other people's brokenness. Where brokenness exists, there is conflict, trauma, and heartbreak.

There are going to be decisions that you have to make regarding a placement—whether to accept it or deny it. Seek peace. You are going to lie down in bed at night carrying the burden of a child's trauma. Seek peace.

Days of doctor visits, school appointments and caseworker check-ins will leave you drained and exhausted. Seek peace.

> **"Foster and adoptive parents feel the weight of other people's brokenness. Where brokenness exists, there is conflict, trauma and heartbreak."**

Somewhere along the way, I learned that peace really isn't a feeling. It's knowing. I *know* that all things work together for the good of those who love Christ and are called according to His purposes (Romans 8:28). I *know* that the peace that passes all understanding is guarding my heart (Philippians 4:7). I *know* that He who began a good work in me is faithful to complete it (Philippians 1:6). As I've sat beside hospital beds, held broken sobbing children in my arms, met birth moms/dads and prayed for lost daughters, I've sought peace. Not a peace that I felt at the moment, but a peace that I know He left with me. Not a peace the world can give me (or understand), but one that tells my worried heart to not be troubled and to not be afraid (John 14:27).

We must remember that the only power fear has over our minds, wills, and emotions is the power we grant it. Practicing peace begins with acknowledging that although we'll face difficulties, God will provide all we need to overcome them. He will use every ounce of sorrow, strife, and pain for His glory and for our good—even though it doesn't feel that way in the moment. Dr. Charles Stanley said, "The God who controls all things—and who is present in your life whether you acknowledge Him or not—is a God of peace. He designed this world with a plan in mind, and it includes *you!*" *You* are a part of His perfect plan in the lives of your children.

Scripture Meditation: Take a few moments to read the following scriptures. Allow the Holy Spirit to speak to your heart about each of them.

Colossians 3:1 (NLT) And let peace that comes from Christ rule in your hearts. For as members of one body you are called to live in peace. And always be thankful.

John 14:27 (NLT) (Jesus' words) I am leaving you with a gift – peace of mind and heart. And the peace I give is a gift the world cannot give. So don't be troubled or afraid.

Romans 8:5–6 (NLT) Those who are dominated by the sinful nature think about sinful things, but those who are controlled by the Holy Spirit think about things that please the Spirit. So letting your sinful nature control your mind leads to death. But letting the Spirit control your mind leads to life and peace.

Ephesians 2:14 (NLT) For Christ himself has brought peace to us. He united Jews and Gentiles into one people when, in his own body on the cross, he broke down the wall of hostility that separated us.

2 Thessalonians 3:16 (NLT) Now may the Lord of peace himself give you peace at all times in every situation. The Lord be with you all.

Capturing Thoughts: Throughout your adoption journey, I encourage you to capture your thoughts, fears, moments of joy, memories, and challenges. It will be a great encouragement to go back and read what you've written. You'll be surprised how much you and your family grow through your experiences.

Prayer Starter: Father, thank you for your gift of peace. Make us carriers of your peace to break away hatred and replace it with love. Give us the insight and wisdom to see difficulty and trust in you for joy in its midst. We ask that you create in us the understanding that we need to bring healing and wholeness to the broken lives you place in our care.

Discussion Questions – Day 13: The Gift of Peace

1. Talk about a time in your life when God seemed silent. As you look back at that time, are you able to see how He was at work? Explain.

2. Do you tend to feel closer to God when your circumstances are good or when they're challenging? Whatever your answer, why do you think that's the case?

3. Read Philippians 4:7. Have you experienced this peace from God that "surpasses all comprehension?" If so, talk about what it was like.

4. What practical things do you do on a regular basis to seek peace?

My Journey:

(Use this space to capture your thoughts, prayers, concerns and questions)

THIS IS HOW ONE SHOULD REGARD US, AS SERVANTS OF CHRIST AND STEWARDS OF THE MYSTERIES OF GOD. MOREOVER, IT IS REQUIRED OF STEWARDS THAT THEY BE FOUND TRUSTWORTHY.

1 CORINTHIANS 4:1–2

DAY 14: TRUSTWORTHY

What God calls us to, He equips us for. And He asks us to be good stewards of what He places in our hands. As foster and adoptive parents we are a vital link between our broken and wounded children and our loving and healing God. It is imperative that we are trustworthy stewards of the responsibilities God gives us.

There will be days that giving up seems logical. These are the times when you must return to the Lord and ask Him for divine intervention and wisdom. You are a miner digging under piles and piles of dirty, broken coal because you know that when you find one little diamond it will be worth all the effort. Our kids' hearts are worth the effort. They must discover that they can rely on you despite their worst behavior. They need to trust that you will be there forever.

We've had to make hard decisions as a family regarding some of our kids. There have been times that their healing journey had to be outside of our house for a season—anywhere from a week to several months. Regardless of the behavior, regardless of the pain, we've had to remind ourselves that we committed to this child and that they *must* trust that we will keep our word. If we've said, "We're with you in this," or "We're going to be your family—

forever," we must mean it, even if that means we're visiting you in a residential treatment facility for a season.

> ## "At the core of a child's ability to adapt and grow in your family is her ability to trust you completely."

At the core of a child's ability to adapt and grow in your family is her ability to trust you completely. Unfortunately, the number one way that she will discover whether you are a person of your word is to *test* you. There are a wide variety of tests, from acting out to shutting down. You must be mindful, prayerful, and wise when handling these tests. Remind yourself that it's likely that no one in the child's life has been dependable. Why should she expect anything different from you?

As followers of Jesus who are seeking to build trust with wounded and vulnerable children, we must also be careful with our words and promises. It's hurtful to both you and the child if you say, "Jesus brought you to our family," and then later ask the caseworker to come get them because their behavior. If a child can't trust you to keep your word, why would she trust Jesus, the One you said brought her to you? Our commitments must run deeper. Our endurance must be greater. Our desire for healing must be unshakable.

Being trustworthy before your kids and before the Lord is something you can do from the start. Your kids' ability to depend on you takes time to develop. Remember that your strength comes from the Lord. One day you want to hear those precious words: "Well done, good and faithful servant!" Until that day, remain as faithful and trustworthy to your kids as your heavenly Father is to you.

Scripture Meditation: Take a few moments to read the following scriptures. Allow the Holy Spirit to speak to your heart about each of them.

Luke 16:10–12 (NLT) If you are faithful in little things, you will be faithful in large ones. But if you are dishonest in little things, you won't be honest with greater responsibilities. And if you are untrustworthy about worldly wealth, who will trust you with the riches of heaven? And if you are not faithful with other people's things, why should you be trusted with things of your own?

2 Samuel 7:28 (NLT) For you are God, O Sovereign Lord. Your words are truth, and you have promised these good things to your servant.

Proverbs 11:13 (NLT) A gossip goes around telling secrets, but those who are trustworthy can keep a confidence.

Ephesians 6:12 (NLT) For we are not fighting against flesh-and-blood enemies, but against rulers and authorities of the unseen world, against mighty powers in this dark world, and against evil spirits in heavenly places.

Capturing Thoughts: Throughout your adoption journey, I encourage you to capture your thoughts, fears, moments of joy, memories, and challenges. It will be a great encouragement to go back and read what you've written. You'll be surprised how much you and your family grow through your experiences.

Prayer Starter: Lord, thank you for entrusting us with your children. Provide us with the wisdom and understanding to reveal your great love and healing to them. Grant us minds like Christ's so we can be faithful and trustworthy, even in the midst of hardship. Help us see the beauty of our children's future through your eyes so we can continually point them toward you.

Discussion Questions – Day 14: Trustworthy

1. What does it mean to be trustworthy? How do you assess another person's trustworthiness?

2. If you have biological children, in what specific ways do they test you? How do you respond?

3. Why is it difficult to follow through when children test us? What practical approaches have you taken to be consistent?

4. Today's devotion says, "If a child can't trust you to keep your word, why would she trust Jesus, the One you said brought her to you?" How does it challenge you?

My Journey:

(Use this space to capture your thoughts, prayers, concerns and questions)

PUT ON THEN, AS GOD'S CHOSEN ONES, HOLY AND BELOVED, COMPASSIONATE

HEARTS, KINDNESS, HUMILITY, MEEKNESS, AND PATIENCE, BEARING WITH ONE

ANOTHER AND, IF ONE HAS A COMPLAINT AGAINST ANOTHER, FORGIVING EACH

OTHER; AS THE LORD HAS FORGIVEN YOU, SO YOU ALSO MUST FORGIVE. AND

ABOVE ALL THESE PUT ON LOVE, WHICH BINDS EVERYTHING TOGETHER IN

PERFECT HARMONY.

COLOSSIANS 3:12-14

DAY 15: ACCEPTANCE

Look up the word acceptance in the dictionary and you'll find a couple definitions: "the action of consenting to receive or undertake something offered," or "the action or process of being received as adequate or suitable." What strikes me is that both sides of the coin are represented here: the healing parent and the wounded child. In both cases—accepting a wounded child and being received as adequate by a healing family—I find miracles.

Parenting a child who was born to someone else is an immense honor, and it's not at all easy. You often have limited or no knowledge, of medical or family history. Or the child's past is so riddled with abuse, it will take him years to heal (and you may not have years with him). Yet Jesus says in Matthew 18:5, "Whoever receives (accepts) a child in my name receives me." There is nothing closer to the heart of God than the heart of the fatherless, the orphan. To parent in the empty space of our own knowledge is to parent *with* God, trusting Him to fill the gaps, to provide understanding, and go before us to make the crooked places straight (Isaiah. 42:16).

> **"In both cases—accepting a wounded child and being received as adequate by a healing family—I find miracles."**

Even if your children were placed with you when they were infants, it can be challenging for them to accept that they are "good enough." Foster care and adoption start with loss. The void left in children separated from their families of birth finds itself filled with feelings of rejection and shame. A child living in your family who wasn't born to you will struggle with natural feelings of being unwanted and unloved. For them, the journey of acceptance—truly understanding that they are adequate and received just as they are—can be long.

Our response as parents is to pray ceaselessly. Seek the heart of God on behalf of those hidden hurts in the hearts of your children. Lovingly address the hard questions every time they come up, even if they've been answered a thousand times before. Your children need ongoing reassurance that you accept them, you *chose* them, and you love them just the way they are.

As you journey together you'll be required to bear with one another in love and operate in forgiveness through behavioral challenges and pain from the past. God brought you together. He has a purpose for this relationship. His great love is the foundation for your family's success. It's this type of forgiving acceptance, this type of love, that binds you together in perfect harmony.

Scripture Meditation: Take a few moments to read the following scriptures. Allow the Holy Spirit to speak to your heart about each of them.

2 Timothy 4:1-2 (NLT) I solemnly urge you in the presence of God and Christ Jesus, who will someday judge the living and the dead when he appears to set up his Kingdom: Preach the word of God. Be prepared, whether the time is favorable or not. Patiently correct, rebuke, and encourage your people with good teaching.

Romans 5:17 (NLT) For the sin of this one man, Adam, caused death to rule over many. But even greater is God's wonderful grace and his gift of righteousness, for all who receive it will live in triumph over sin and death through this one man, Jesus Christ.

Matthew 9:11–12 (NLT) But when the Pharisees saw this, they asked his disciples, "Why does your teacher eat with such scum?" When Jesus heard this, he said, "Healthy people don't need a doctor – sick people do."

Matthew 25:40 (NLT) And the King will say, 'I tell you the truth, when you did it to one of the least of these my brothers and sisters, you were doing it to me."

Capturing Thoughts: Throughout your adoption journey, I encourage you to capture your thoughts, fears, moments of joy, memories, and challenges. It will be a great encouragement to go back and read what you've written. You'll be surprised how much you and your family grow through your experiences.

Prayer Starter: Lord, thank you for moving our hearts and giving us compassion, kindness, humility, meekness, and patience so we can bear with our children, love them, and forgive them when they act out of their hurt. Grant us wisdom to show them that they are valuable, loved, and accepted. We know that, through you, we will bond in perfect harmony.

Discussion Questions – Day 15: Acceptance

1. Talk about someone who has loved you unconditionally. How did that person's love affect the way you view yourself?

2. Read Matthew 25:31-40. Does this passage give you a different perspective on foster care and adoption? Explain.

3. Today's devotion says, "A child living in your family who wasn't born to you will struggle with natural feelings of being unwanted and unloved. For them, the journey of acceptance – truly understanding that they are adequate and received just as they are – can be long. " Respond to that statement. Do you tend to want to run toward or away from the challenge described?

4. Take time to share any concerns that you have about your ability to accept a child that isn't your own.

My Journey:

(Use this space to capture your thoughts, prayers, concerns and questions)

FOR MY FATHER AND MY MOTHER HAVE FORSAKEN ME,

BUT THE LORD WILL TAKE ME IN.

PSALM 27:10

DAY 16: DEALING WITH REJECTION

People reject others because of their own feelings of rejection. This is especially true of wounded children. Whether placed with an adoptive or foster family at birth or when they're older, children's sense of rejection can affect their relationships for a lifetime. They need to be taught how to understand and deal with feelings of rejection.

Rejection in foster and adoptive parent–child relationships can be a major trigger for disruption and dissatisfaction because both parent and child react to it. In my own journey, I've found that the root of rejection in my children is often a trigger for my own feelings of rejection. Because I have experienced abandonment and rejection in my own life, my feelings can be easily hurt when I perceive that my children are rejecting me. The thing I understand most—their natural feelings of rejection—is the thing that can hurt me and make me angry fastest. After all, I'm trying to do good by providing them with a home, love, and encouragement. Why on earth would they reject that?

It's easy to enter this journey feeling like we are heroes rescuing children from horrors such as homelessness, sex trafficking, poverty, prison and abuse. While those possibilities do exist in the trajectory of our children's future, only God can know what would have occurred without us. Children don't feel rescued. They feel rejected. In their minds, the people who should love them the most in this world wouldn't or couldn't care for them. That's a bitter pill to swallow, and as their parents, we should never forget the depth of this void.

> ## "Even though adding another child to your family is a happy event for you, the child doesn't necessarily feel that way."

Wanting our children to be happy for all of the things we've provided for them is a challenge we all face. We want them to appreciate and return our love. It's extremely hard when they don't. We have to remind ourselves that their distress has nothing to do with us; it's not personal. Healing takes time—lots of time.

Even though adding another child to your family is a happy event for you, the child doesn't necessarily feel that way. Sometimes, no matter how lovingly you talk about fostering and adopting, an unspoken root of rejection exists within the child. When you tell your child that you "chose" her, you communicate an unspoken truth that her birth parents didn't. That may sound harsh, but it's what children experience. Those feelings can have a major impact on a child's view of herself and her value.

The only way to deal with rejection in foster care and adoption is to ask God to reveal any area in your life where bitterness, resentment, or loss has a grip. It could be related to infertility or your own abandonment issues. Not dealing with your own feelings of rejection and finding healing before you become a foster or adoptive parent can trigger significant unexpected turmoil later as you face issues with your child.

Scripture Meditation: Take a few moments to read the following scriptures. Allow the Holy Spirit to speak to your heart about each of them.

John 1:11 (NLT) He came to his own people, and even they rejected him.

Psalm 34:17–20 (NLT) The Lord hears his people when they call to him for help. He rescues them from all their troubles. The Lord is close to the brokenhearted; he rescues those whose spirits are crushed. The righteous person faces many troubles, but the Lord comes to the rescue each time. For the Lord protects the bones of the righteous; not one of them is broken!

2 Corinthians 12:9 (NLT) Each time he said, "My grace is all you need. My power works best in weakness." So now I am glad to boast about my weaknesses, so that the power of Christ can work through me.

Psalm 66:16–20 (NLT) Come and listen, all you who fear God, and I will tell you what he did for me. For I cried out to him to help, praising him as I spoke. If I had not confessed the sin in my heart, the Lord would not have listened. But God did listen! He paid attention to my prayer. Praise God, who did not ignore my prayer or withdraw his unfailing love from me.

Capturing Thoughts: Throughout your adoption journey, I encourage you to capture your thoughts, fears, moments of joy, memories, and challenges. It will be a great encouragement to go back and read what you've written. You'll be surprised how much you and your family grow through your experiences.

Prayer Starter: Lord, reveal in our hearts any hidden hurts and wounds that you want us to deal with, so we can accomplish your will in the lives of our children. Give us wisdom in the area of rejection so we can be your hands and feet of healing in our children's lives.

Discussion Questions – Day 16: Dealing With Rejection

1. Talk about a time when you've felt rejected. How did that experience affect your relationship with the person that rejected you?

2. Today's devotion says, "We reject others because of our own feelings of rejection." How have you seen that pattern play out in your own life?

3. Have you asked God to reveal any areas in your life where bitterness, resentment, or loss has a grip? If so, what steps have you taken to begin to loosen that grip? If not, why?

4. What is one thing you can do to begin to prepare your heart for the possibility that a child you bring into your home may reject you? How can this group help you?

My Journey:

(Use this space to capture your thoughts, prayers, concerns and questions)

FOR AM I NOW SEEKING THE APPROVAL OF MAN, OR OF GOD? OR AM I TRYING
TO PLEASE MAN? IF I WERE STILL TRYING TO PLEASE MAN, I WOULD NOT BE A
SERVANT OF CHRIST.

GALATIANS 1:10

DAY 17: THE PRAISE OF MEN

Orphan care is a major issue in our world today. Awareness matters. It requires moms and dads willing to speak out on behalf of the orphan. Our world needs to see those of us who've chosen to care for foster and adoptive children as successful and blessed in our foster or adoptive journeys. We need to share our stories of blessing, our moments of despair and the miracles that we've seen God do in our families. Yet, this very important need can also be an area where the enemy can trip us up. We have to guard ourselves against placing the praise of men above the glory of God in our journey.

We should be careful of the spotlight on our families—for our sake and for our children's. First, our children's stories are theirs to tell. We must guard the story of how they joined our family carefully. Other people are going to be naturally curious, and we are naturally proud to be their mom and dad. Nonetheless, putting your child on the spot by asking them to answer uncomfortable questions or sharing personal details can totally derail your efforts to connect with them and gain their trust. Just as we can't think of ourselves as heroes, we also can't allow others to place us on the hero pedestal either. Orphan care isn't a call to heroism it's a call to humility and brokenness.

Early in our journey, I taught classes on adoptive parenting because, by the grace of God, we were blessed and successful. I would hear things like, "You're such a good mom," "I don't know how you do it," and "I wish my kids would adjust like yours." Then one of my daughters ran away from home. Suddenly and very publicly, I was a mom in crisis. The enemy invaded my thoughts. I found myself worrying about what everyone was thinking about my parenting.

"What others think" is a real battle in the mind of every parent,— adoptive, foster and biological alike. Our kids are a reflection of who we are. When they misbehave, our minds run to what others think rather than what's best for our kids. The root of this "praise of men" trap is fear. We fear rejection by others. We fear losing status. We fear being talked about. But the only fear we're instructed to walk in is the *fear of the Lord.*

> **"Reminding ourselves that we're not to seek the praise of man, but the glory of God gives us the freedom to let God shape our kids however He sees fit."**

Our children aren't trophies. They are children. Kids are kids, teens are teens, young adults are young adults—they will make mistakes, bite, kick, throw toys, lie, run away, smoke, drink, wreck the car, and steal. Kids have done those things for generations. Reminding ourselves that we're not to seek the praise of man but the glory of God gives us the freedom to let God shape our kids however He sees fit. We need to get out of the way, trust Him, and love them. Who cares what others say?

Scripture Meditation: Take a few moments to read the following scriptures. Allow the Holy Spirit to speak to your heart about each of them.

Proverbs 29:25 (NLT) Fearing people is a dangerous trap, but trusting the Lord means safety.

1 Thessalonians 2:4 (NLT) For we speak as messengers approved by God to be entrusted with the Good News. Our purpose is to please God, not people. He alone examines the motives of our heart.

Isaiah 2:22 (NLT) Don't put your trust in mere humans. They are as frail as breath. What good are they?

2 Corinthians 5:9 (NLT) So whether we are here in this body or away from this body, our goal is to please Him.

Galatians 6:1–8 (NLT) Dear brothers and sisters, if another believer is overcome by some sin, you who are godly should gently and humbly help that person back onto the right path. And be careful not to fall into the same temptation yourself.

Capturing Thoughts: Throughout your adoption journey, I encourage you to capture your thoughts, fears, moments of joy, memories, and challenges. It will be a great encouragement to go back and read what you've written. You'll be surprised how much you and your family grow through your experiences.

Prayer Starter: Father, thank you for not being ashamed of us when we fail—no matter how far we run or how hard we fall. Your loving arms are always there to catch us. Show us how to be like you with our children. Teach us to give grace and to fear you, so our kids can become all you've created them to be.

Discussion Questions – Day 17: The Praise of Men

1. Talk about a time when you received praise from people because of the gifts and talents God has given you. How was that praise helpful? How was it harmful?

2. Have you ever judged another parent based on his or her child's public behavior? Why do you think we're quick to assume the worst of others?

3. Imagine your child is acting out or having a public meltdown. How much would you be concerned with how others view you because of your child's behavior? How do you think that concern would affect your ability to parent effectively?

4. Read Galatians 1:10. What is one thing you can do to focus your attention on God's approval and away from other people's? What can this group do to support you?

My Journey:

(Use this space to capture your thoughts, prayers, concerns and questions)

FOR EVEN THE SON OF MAN DID NOT COME TO BE SERVED, BUT TO SERVE, AND

GIVE HIS LIFE AS A RANSOM FOR MANY.

MARK 10:45

DAY 18: SERVANTHOOD

Jesus was intentional about serving. His entire mission on Earth was to serve, to pour himself out on our behalf. The sports phrase "leave it all on the field" comes to mind when I consider what Jesus did for us—He left it all on the cross. As followers of Jesus, we are to do the same. When we give Jesus his rightful place as Lord of our lives, His lordship is expressed in how we serve others.

Like Jesus, our mission includes pouring ourselves out for others. To empty ourselves is to lay aside our comfort, routine, and plans in order to love and serve others so that Jesus might be made strong in them through our example. This type of servant-leadership is exactly what's required of us as foster and adoptive parents.

As you deal with challenges and struggles with your children, remind yourself of your primary goal as a parent: you are the hands and feet of Jesus in their lives. It is your responsibility to lead them to Him. You do that by being a reflection of Him. My pastor, Dennis Rouse, once said, "You never know when you are the only link in a person's life to Jesus. Don't take that lightly." I've never forgotten that. I remind myself of it often . . . especially when I feel like giving up.

As a mom of children from hard places, I can't tell you how many times I've had to remind myself of Jesus – naked, beaten and mocked on the Cross. In many moments when a child that I've done my best to love unconditionally is mocking my efforts, berating me behind my back to others and saying spiteful things about our family, I've been tempted to fight back and defend myself. In some cases, I have—much to my regret. But, in the times I've successfully avoided unnecessary conflict, it's because I know that Jesus endured the pain of the cross because He believes I am worth it, even though I am continually ungrateful and disobedient. Each and every one of my children is worth it. They are worth every tear, every sacrifice, every prayer, and every moment. I don't want them to see a perfect parent when they look at me. I want them to see their Lord and Savior Jesus Christ and know that—no matter what—He thinks they are worth it all.

> **"I don't want them to see a perfect parent when they look at me. I want them to see their Lord and Savior Jesus Christ and know that—no matter what—He thinks they are worth it all."**

Parenting with a servant's heart isn't easy. It doesn't mean we do everything for our kids without teaching them how to be responsible for themselves. But the day after a difficult interaction with a birth parent or trouble at school with another student may not be the right time to push the point about your child forgetting to take the trash out *again*. Instead, it might be the perfect opportunity to ask your son or daughter to walk outside with you as you take out the trash because you want to take a little time to speak love into his or her life.

When the homework is overwhelming, the same issue has arisen for the hundredth time, or you've just been lied to again, finding that place in your heart to serve takes effort, but the payoff is worth it. Seeing our children through their challenges and showing them by example how to serve others in love is how they see, hear, and feel their Savior. It's why He chose you to be their parent.

Scripture Meditation: Take a few moments to read the following scriptures. Allow the Holy Spirit to speak to your heart about each of them.

Mark 9:35 (NLT) He sat down, called the twelve disciples over to him, and said, "Whoever wants to be first must take last place and be the servant of everyone else."

1 Peter 4:10 (NLT) God has given each of you a gift from his great variety of spiritual gifts. Use them well to serve one another.

John 15:12–13 (NLT) This is my commandment: Love each other in the same way I have loved you. There is no greater love than to lay down one's life for one's friends.

Philippians 2:6–7 (NLT) Though he was God, he did not think of equality with God as something to cling to. Instead, he gave up his divine privileges; he took the humble position of a slave and was born as a human being.

Capturing Thoughts: Throughout your adoption journey, I encourage you to capture your thoughts, fears, moments of joy, memories, and challenges. It will be a great encouragement to go back and read what you've written. You'll be surprised how much you and your family grow through your experiences.

Prayer Starter: Lord, thank you for being the perfect servant-leader for us. Give us your divine wisdom as we prepare to parent our children. Show us how to serve them for your glory. When we feel frustrated, remind us to trust you and turn to you.

Discussion Questions – Day 18: Servanthood

1. Talk about a person who was the hands and feet of Jesus in your life. How did that person lead you by serving you? How did his or her humility change the course of your life?

2. Read John 13:3-9. Notice Peter's reaction to Jesus. What are some reasons it can be difficult for us to allow ourselves to be served? Why does being served make us uncomfortable?

3. Why is the call to serve so challenging? What worries do you have about your ability to serve children under your care?

4. Read 1 Peter 4:10. What gifts has God given you that make you uniquely qualified to serve adoptive or foster children?

My Journey:

(Use this space to capture your thoughts, prayers, concerns and questions)

AND WHY IS THIS GRANTED TO ME THAT THE

MOTHER OF MY LORD SHOULD COME TO ME?

LUKE 1:43

DAY 19: HUMILITY

I often feel as Elizabeth must have in that moment when her cousin Mary approached her. *"Why is this granted to me?"* Who am I that God chose me to be a mom to His girls? Who am I that He found me capable of caring for those who are so precious to Him? This is the foundation of humility: an understanding that apart from God we are nothing. Without Him we can do nothing. When I consider the enormity of the task that God has set before me, I have no other reaction but *"Why me, God? Who am I?"*

Humility is critical in my life as a mom. When I fail, the root of my failure is usually an absence of humility. Sometimes I think I have the answer because I've spent so much time educating myself about the issues of wounded children. Then my solution is an utter failure. When I evaluate the situation, I realize that either I never asked God for His answer or I didn't submit my struggle and solution to wise counsel. Doing both requires humility. I have to humble myself and admit that I'm struggling and unsure what to do.

Parenting a child through foster care and adoption often puts your family and parenting under a microscope. People are naturally curious about the dynamics of your family. Sometimes your children's behaviors and social skills will draw extra attention to you. Others will offer their advice, critique and opinions—even when you didn't ask. There are going to be plenty of people who think they know how to parent and love your kids better than you do. I've had to learn how to listen, be gracious and trust the Lord to give me wisdom and direction.

I remember a situation with one of our girls that resulted in several other adults coming into the picture to help us navigate decisions. There were varying opinions about our initial handling of the behavior, ideas about what to do now and even a few attacks on us in general. It was a tough moment. I found myself silently praying and asking God to give me grace, help me understand the point of view of others and ultimately direct our steps. Trust me, finding the ability to be humble in a moment where you feel judged and attacked is hard. In the end, I walked away with some new ideas and new friends. If I had been prideful, dismissive or defensive the situation would have turned out vastly different.

> **"Trust me, finding the ability to be humble in a moment where you feel judged and attached is hard."**

1 Peter 5:6 says, *"Humble yourselves therefore under the mighty hand of God, that he may exalt you in due time."* The interesting thing is that in the preceding verses, Peter gives instructions to the "overseers" of the church—those entrusted to shepherd and care for the children of God. He instructs them to serve willingly, not for personal benefit, to be an example to those they shepherd because in these things comes the crown of glory from the Lord which will not fade away. We are called to serve those that God entrusts into our care, which includes our children.

The desire to "do it on my own" is a matter of pride. It's a desire to be independent. It's a desire to be seen as strong and capable. We must learn to walk in humility and understand that even though God has chosen us as the "overseers" of our children, He has a lot to say to us about how we parent them. He placed others in our lives that have wisdom and understanding to share with us. We have a lot to learn, if we humble ourselves, ask, and listen.

Scripture Meditation: Take a few moments to read the following scriptures. Allow the Holy Spirit to speak to your heart about each of them.

Psalms 149:4 (NLT) For the Lord delights in his people; he crowns the humble with victory.

Proverbs 11:2 (NLT) Pride leads to disgrace, but with humility comes wisdom.

Philippians 2:5–8 (NLT) You must have the same attitude that Christ Jesus had. Though he was God, he did not think of equality with God as something to cling to. Instead, he gave up his divine privileges; he took the humble position of a slave and was born as a human being. When he appeared in human for, he humbled himself in obedience to God and died a criminal's death on a cross.

Psalms 25:9 (NLT) He leads the humble in doing right, teaching them his way.

Capturing Thoughts: Throughout your adoption journey, I encourage you to capture your thoughts, fears, moments of joy, memories, and challenges. It will be a great encouragement to go back and read what you've written. You'll be surprised how much you and your family grow through your experiences.

Prayer Starter: Lord, create humble hearts in us. Thank you for choosing us for this journey. Surround us with people that are wise in counsel and understanding. Give us the ability to honor and value their wisdom. Be quick to show us when arrogance or pride rises in our hearts.

Discussion Questions – Day 19: Humility

1. Have you ever met a truly humble person? If so, what was it like to be in that person's presence?

2. Today's devotion says, "This is the foundation of humility: an understanding that apart from God we are nothing. Without Him we can do nothing." When is it easy for you to grasp that truth? When is it difficult?

3. You probably entered into adoption or foster care because God has gifted you in ways that make you a natural fit for that ministry and mission. What are some things you can do to be intentional about depending on God even in areas where you're most tempted to try doing it on your own?

My Journey:

(Use this space to capture your thoughts, prayers, concerns and questions)

AND AFTER YOU HAVE SUFFERED A LITTLE WHILE,

THE GOD OF ALL GRACE, WHO HAS CALLED YOU TO

HIS ETERNAL GLORY IN CHRIST, WILL HIMSELF RESTORE,

CONFIRM, STRENGTHEN, AND ESTABLISH YOU.

1 PETER 5:10

DAY 20: INNER HEALING

Infertility. Miscarriage. Death of a child. A previous failed adoption. A history that includes verbal or sexual abuse. These are losses we experience. If they're not properly healed, they can negatively affect our foster and adoption journeys. We must carefully and prayerfully consider areas within our hearts that we haven't given to God for healing. We have to give ourselves the freedom to grieve.

Too often, parents who have unresolved loss in their lives enter the adoption process with a hidden hole. Worse yet, they expect the child's presence to fill that hole. That expectation is unrealistic, especially when placed on children suffering trauma and loss.

I've had to work through this in my own life. I suffered two miscarriages prior to having our first child, almost died giving birth and was told I could never have more children. It was a struggle for me for years. After our foster care and adoption journey began, I quickly realized that my dream of what life would be like with multiple children was blocking me from enjoying the reality of what life was like with the daughters that God had brought me. For years I had imagined what life would be like with a larger family, multiple daughters and siblings for Kristan. I envisioned talking, sharing, laughing and being a family. While those things did occur, a lot of things that I hadn't envisioned came with it—fighting, hurtful words and children who didn't want to be a part of our family. It took me a long time to realize that my expectations for what family life was supposed to look like were unrealistic— especially when parenting a child with such great trauma and loss.

> "...my expectations for what family life was supposed to look like were unrealistic—especially when parenting a child with such great trauma and loss."

Another area of loss that I've been forced to confront is my own broken family background. There were many hurts in my childhood—some that still need to be resolved today. These play out for me through my tendency to overcompensate for what I feel like I didn't have growing up. When I do something for or with my children that I never had growing up and they don't notice or don't appreciate it, I get angry and hurt. It took me a while to realize that these feelings weren't coming from my current situation. Instead they were a result of pain I had experienced decades before. Our children can't make up for the experiences, losses and hurts we've suffered. They can't heal those wounds—it's not their place. Like me, many will find that their journey as a foster and adoptive parent lands them in therapy for themselves. To be honest, I probably should have gone long ago.

When we experience loss, it can make us angry with God. *Why did you let this happen to me? What have I done to deserve this?* We sometimes direct unresolved anger towards God at our children, especially during vulnerable moments when they touch a raw nerve. A child screaming, "You can't do anything right," "I wish you were never my mom," or "There's a reason God didn't let you have a child," are triggers that can expose your carefully hidden pain.

The good news is that God is a redeemer and healer. He wants to bring light and love to the painful areas in your life. And here's the best part: when God heals and redeems your pain, it becomes the strength you need to help your child heal. The pain you've experienced may help you to enter into your child's pain. Understanding your own dark place will help you guide him to the light.

Scripture Meditation: Take a few moments to read the following scriptures. Allow the Holy Spirit to speak to your heart about each of them.

> **Psalms 34:17–20** (NLT) The Lord hears his people when they call to him for help. He rescues them from all their troubles. The Lord is close to the brokenhearted; he rescues those whose spirits are crushed. The righteous person faces many troubles, but the Lord comes to the rescue each time. For the Lord protects the bones of the righteous; not one of them is broken!

> **Psalm 147:3** (NLT) He heals the brokenhearted and bandages their wounds.

> **Romans 8:15–16** (NLT) So you have not received a spirit that makes you fearful slaves. Instead, you received God's Spirit when he adopted you as his own children. Now we call him, "Abba Father."

For his Spirit joins with our spirit to affirm that we are God's children.

Isaiah 54:17 (NLT) But in that coming day no weapon turned against you will succeed. You will silence every voice. These benefits are enjoyed by the servants of the Lord; their vindication will come from me. I, the Lord, have spoken!

Psalms 30:11 (NLT) You have turned my morning into joyful dancing. You have taken away my clothes of mourning and clothed me with joy.

Capturing Thoughts: Throughout your adoption journey, I encourage you to capture your thoughts, fears, moments of joy, memories, and challenges. It will be a great encouragement to go back and read what you've written. You'll be surprised how much you and your family grow through your experiences.

Prayer Starter: Father, I give all of my heart to you. Examine the deep places within me. Show me any area I've hidden from you out of anger, hurt, or fear. Bring it to light so I can be a light of love to my child.

Discussion Questions – Day 20: Inner Healing

1. What are some things your children or others do that really get under your skin? Why do you think those behaviors bother you so much?

2. Have you ever been angry with God? How did that anger affect your relationships with other people?

3. Read Psalm 34:18. What do you think it means for God to be close to the brokenhearted? What comfort does that provide in your own circumstances?

4. Do you need to deal with unresolved loss? If so, what is your best next step? How can this group help you take that step?

My Journey:

(Use this space to capture your thoughts, prayers, concerns and questions)

FINALLY, BE STRONG IN THE LORD AND IN THE STRENGTH OF HIS MIGHT. PUT ON THE WHOLE ARMOR OF GOD, THAT YOU MAY BE ABLE TO STAND AGAINST THE SCHEMES OF THE DEVIL. FOR WE DO NOT WRESTLE AGAINST FLESH AND BLOOD, BUT AGAINST THE RULERS & AUTHORITIES IN HIGH PLACES.

EPHESIANS 6:10-12

DAY 21: RELEASING CONTROL

Issues of control are like spiritual battles (in most cases, they *are* spiritual battles): what we fight about on the surface isn't the real issue. The real issues are insecurity, loss, and distrust. Imagine having the course of your life decided by complete strangers. That's what adopted and foster care children experience. That's why they fight for control. It's a fight that only produces frustration, doubt, and fatigue.

> **"A battle for control is a losing battle for both of you. You lose peace. Your child loses an opportunity to learn trust."**

A battle for control is a losing battle for both of you. You lose peace. Your child loses an opportunity to learn trust. Battling is exhausting for both of you. Learn to let go in the little things. Relax. Allowing your child to win sometimes in an atmosphere of peace and trust is a win for you too.

Control battles with foster and adopted children can erupt from the most seemingly insignificant things—what to wear, what to eat or having to do a chore. As parents, we have to learn how to determine when a child is just simply trying to control because they've never had it, or just being defiant. We are far too quick to label a refusal to do something as defiance instead of trying to see deeper. We have to learn the art of the win-win with our kids —I get obedience (win for me) and you get to feel in control (win for you).

One of the most powerful tools in the battle of control is choice. Save the demands for the really important stuff —you *don't* have a choice about going to school, but you *do* have a choice about what you eat for breakfast and what color jacket you wear. Learn how to guide your children to the right decisions by giving them several right choices. For example, if you want your child to wear a coat to school and wearing a coat is your ultimate win, it doesn't really matter if they choose the red, blue or green one—even if it doesn't match their outfit.

Trust in the Lord for His guidance. Trust Him to direct your words and actions. When you find yourself in the battle of control, ask yourself if this issue really matters. And never forget that our real battle is not with flesh and blood. Prayer changes everything.

Rely on the Lord for wisdom and creativity. Allow your children freedom in areas where it's safe for them to be in control. Make it a habit to give them choices instead of commands: "I need you to take out the trash, would you like to do it now or after dinner?" Letting them choose is a win for both of you. The chore gets done *and* they experience control. This creates trust and peace in your home. The ultimate win.

Scripture Meditation: Take a few moments to read the following scriptures. Allow the Holy Spirit to speak to your heart about each of them.

Romans 8:28 (NLT) And we know that God causes everything to work together for the good of those who love God and are called according to His purpose for them.

Matthew 19:26 (NLT) Jesus looked at them intently and said, "Humanly speaking, it is impossible. But with God everything is possible."

Isaiah 55:8–11 (NLT) "My thoughts are nothing like your thoughts," says the Lord, "And my ways are far beyond anything you could imagine. For just as the heavens are higher than the earth, so my ways are higher than your ways and my thoughts higher than your thoughts. The rain and snow come down from the heavens and stay on the ground to water the earth. They cause the grain to grow, producing seed for the farmer and bread for the hungry. It is the same with my Word. I send it out, and it always produces fruit. It will accomplish all I want it to, and it will prosper where I send it."

Psalm 55:22 (NLT) Give your burdens to the Lord, and he will take care of you. He will not permit the godly to slip and fall.

Luke 1:37 (NLT) For nothing is impossible with God.

Capturing Thoughts: Throughout your adoption journey, I encourage you to capture your thoughts, fears, moments of joy, memories, and challenges. It will be a great encouragement to go back and read what you've written. You'll be surprised how much you and your family grow through your experiences.

Prayer Starter: Father, give us wisdom to recognize control issues and the ability to respond with love and patience. As your hands and feet to our children, give us the strength to guide them to trust us as their parents and you as their heavenly Father.

Discussion Questions – Day 21: Releasing Control

1. Think about a time in your life when you didn't have control over your circumstances. What did you feel? How did you respond?

2. Today's devotion says, "Allowing your child to win sometimes in an atmosphere of peace and trust is a win for you too." What are some ways you can tell when a battle with your child isn't worth fighting?

3. Read Romans 8:28. How do you think this applies to your call to help orphans or foster children?

4. What are some practical things you can do to submit to God and allow Him to direct your words and actions?

Pam Parish

My Journey:

(Use this space to capture your thoughts, prayers, concerns and questions)

FOR YOU CREATED MY INMOST BEING; YOU KNIT ME TOGETHER IN MY MOTHER'S WOMB. I PRAISE YOU BECAUSE I AM FEARFULLY AND WONDERFULLY MADE; YOUR WORKS ARE WONDERFUL, I KNOW THAT FULL WELL. MY FRAME WAS NOT HIDDEN FROM YOU WHEN I WAS MADE IN THE SECRET PLACE. WHEN I WAS WOVEN TOGETHER IN THE DEPTHS OF THE EARTH, YOUR EYES SAW MY UNFORMED BODY. ALL THE DAYS ORDAINED FOR ME WERE WRITTEN IN YOUR BOOK BEFORE ONE OF THEM CAME TO BE.

PSALM 139:13-16

DAY 22: THE VALUE OF LIFE

At the moment of conception, each human life is given a spirit and purpose by our Creator. Galatians 1:15 says God knew us even before he formed us in our mother's wombs, and he set us apart with a purpose. To the core of our being, we must believe that because it is the thing we have to fight for in the lives of our children.

Being given up for adoption, abandoned or removed from your home all bring with them heavy doses of insecurity for children. *"Did my mom/dad not love me enough to keep me… protect me…..stay?"* These types of questions often haunt children's minds causing them to question their value and worth. If a parent committed physical or sexual abuse or knowingly allowed it to happen, it creates a lasting sense of unworthiness in children. These deep-seeded questions about worth live within our children's minds and produce devaluing messages of shame that are hard to overcome without consistent, loving, and understanding parenting.

119

In moments when our children's behaviors are at their worst, we have to remind ourselves of their eternal value. Everyone is worth it in the eyes of God. Yet, in our most exhausted moments, we often ask ourselves, "Is it all even worth it?" Let me help you answer. YES! YES! YES! It IS worth it. Every child is worth it.

All life is God-breathed. We are all image-bearers of our Creator. That gives every life infinite value and worth. Our adversary, the devil, wants to steal, kill, and destroy. The first thing he attacks is our sense of value. He has had temporary victory in our children's lives. He has damaged their self-image. But we know Jesus came to restore and redeem us all from the curse.

> **"Seeing the eternal value of our children is critical in moments of difficulty and doubt."**

God has given us dominion over the works of the enemy. He has given us the power of healing through the Holy Spirit. He has equipped us to be the hands and feet of Jesus for our children. We must choose to live out that power through acts of love, words of affirmation, guidance, correction, and faith that our children will one day become all that God has created them to be. Seeing the eternal value of our children is critical in moments of difficulty and doubt. It enables us to see through the patterns of trauma, anger, and loss that we walk through alongside them.

Scripture Meditation: Take a few moments to read the following scriptures. Allow the Holy Spirit to speak to your heart about each of them.

Galatians 1:15 (NLT) But even before I was born, God chose me and called me by his marvelous grace.

John 10:10 (NLT) The thief's purpose is to steal, kill and destroy. My purpose is to give them a rich and satisfying life.

2 Corinthians 5:17 (NLT) This means that anyone who belongs to Christ has become a new person. The old life is gone; a new life has begun!

Galatians 3:26, 28–29 (NLT) For you are all children of God through faith in Christ Jesus. There is no longer Jew or Gentile, slave or free, male and female. For you are all one in Christ Jesus. And now that you belong to Christ, you are the true children of Abraham. You are his heirs, and God's promises to Abraham belong to you.

Capturing Thoughts: Throughout your adoption journey, I encourage you to capture your thoughts, fears, moments of joy, memories, and challenges. It will be a great encouragement to go back and read what you've written. You'll be surprised how much you and your family grow through your experiences.

Prayer Starter: Father, thank you for giving me life and creating me in your image. I know you've knit my child together with purpose and destiny. Give me wisdom to show my child her value. Help me show her that no matter what has happened before she became mine, she is a person of beauty and infinite worth. She is your child and deserves love, respect, and dignity.

Discussion Questions – Day 22: The Value of Life

1. In what ways would you view yourself differently if you took it to heart that you are an image-bearer of God?

2. In what ways would you view and treat others differently if you took it to heart that they are image-bearers of God?

3. Read the NIV version of John 10:10. What do you think Jesus means when He says that He came that we may "have life and have it to the full?" What implications does that statement have for your daily life?

4. What practical things can you do to remind yourself on a daily basis that the children in your care are image-bearers of God? How can this group support you?

My Journey:

(Use this space to capture your thoughts, prayers, concerns and questions)

THEREFORE, I URGE YOU, BROTHERS, IN VIEW OF GOD'S MERCY, TO OFFER

YOUR BODIES AS LIVING SACRIFICES, HOLY AND PLEASING TO GOD—THIS IS

YOUR SPIRITUAL ACT OF WORSHIP...FOR BY THE GRACE GIVEN ME I SAY TO

EVERY ONE OF YOU: DO NOT THINK OF YOURSELF MORE HIGHLY THAN YOU

OUGHT, BUT RATHER THINK OF YOURSELF WITH SOBER JUDGMENT...

ROMANS 12:1-3

DAY 23: A LIVING SACRIFICE

Paul instructs us in Romans to give ourselves to God as sacrifices, holy and pleasing, because it is an act of worship to do so. If you read all of Romans 12, you'll find that being a living sacrifice before God means being humble, loving completely, having patience, using the gifts God gave you to the best of your ability, and reaching out to those in need with genuine compassion.

Each time you tend to your child's unique needs— counseling, medical challenges, behavior challenges, and more—every action becomes a living sacrifice, holy and beautiful before God. None of us are too good to lie in bed beside a broken, crying child. There isn't a single day that God doesn't see you cleaning soiled sheets, picking up broken glass or visiting a lost child in a youth detention center that He doesn't see a heart that's turned toward Him and smiles.

> **"There is nothing broken beyond His ability to repair, not a single ash that He can't make beautiful."**

Everyone who meets me and finds out that I have seven daughters and three grandchildren is shocked. Nearly without fail they say I am too young to be a grandmother. When I entered this journey there's no way that I could have imagined that I would have three grandchildren by the time I attended my first graduation ceremony. Yet in the brokenness of this journey, three little lives have joined ours and they are truly beautiful. Hearing those sweet voices say "Nana" brings a joy to my heart that's a healing balm for the rocky path that brought them to me. There is nothing broken beyond His ability to repair, not a single ash that He can't make beautiful.

As God has called you to become a mother or father to the fatherless—He has equipped you with the measure of faith required for the journey. It is your responsibility to dig into His Word every day, renew your mind, and receive new mercies for that day. God's Word is the only power on earth that is eternally transformational. It is through His word that you will receive the confidence of His miraculous power to heal and restore your children.

We are to rejoice in the hope He has given us for our children, be patient in the trials that come our way, and persist in prayer so that we may hear and know His will. What happened to our children before we came into their lives is the result of living in a fallen world.

God promises good will overcome evil. Through Jesus, evil has already been defeated. Remaining faithful in parenting our children is a pure and undefiled act of worship before our heavenly Father. It is a living sacrifice.

Scripture Meditation: Take a few moments to read the following scriptures. Allow the Holy Spirit to speak to your heart about each of them.

Romans 12 (read entire chapter)

2 Timothy 3:16 (NLT) All scripture is inspired by God and is useful to teach us what is true and to make us realize what is wrong in our lives. It corrects us when we are wrong and teaches us to do right.

Romans 6:12–13 (NLT) Don't let sin control the way you live; do not give into your sinful desires. Do not let any part of your body become an instrument of evil to serve sin. Instead, give yourselves completely to God, for you were dead, but now you have a new life. So use your whole body as an instrument to do what is right for the glory of God.

Romans 8:11–13 (NLT) The Spirit of God, who raised Jesus from the dead, lives in you. And just as God raised Christ Jesus from the dead, he will give life to your mortal bodies by this same Spirit living in you. Therefore, dear brothers and sisters, you have no obligation to do what your sinful nature urges you to do. For if you live by dictates, you will die. But if through the power of the Spirit you put to death the deeds of your sinful nature, you will live.

Psalms 1:2–3 (NLT) But they delight in the law of the Lord, meditating on it day and night. They are like trees planted along the riverbank, bearing fruit each season. Their leaves never wither, and they prosper in all they do.

Capturing Thoughts: Throughout your adoption journey, I encourage you to capture your thoughts, fears, moments of joy, memories, and challenges. It will be a great encouragement to go back and read what you've written. You'll be surprised how much you and your family grow through your experiences.

Prayer Starter: Father, may my life and my parenting be a living sacrifice pleasing to you. Thank you for your Word, which I can use daily to cleanse, direct, and rejuvenate myself for the journey ahead.

Discussion Questions – Day 23: A Living Sacrifice

1. Raising children is exhausting. What are some things you can do to recharge?

2. Think about a time when God called you to do something difficult. How did you respond? How did your response influence your relationship with your Heavenly Father?

3. What practical things can you do to prepare yourself to do difficult, tiring work with joy?

4. Today's devotion says, "…being a living sacrifice before God means being humble, loving completely, having patience, using the gifts God gave you to the best of your ability, and reaching out to those in need with genuine compassion." Which of these areas is most difficult for you? What is one thing you can do to focus on that area?

Pam Parish

My Journey:

(Use this space to capture your thoughts, prayers, concerns and questions)

So he got up from the meal, took off his outer clothing, and wrapped a towel around His waist. After that, he poured water into a basin and began to wash His disciples feet, drying them with the towel that was wrapped around Him.

John 13:4–5

DAY 24: WASHING FEET

In Jesus' day, washing feet was a duty reserved for the lowest of servants. But Jesus, King of Kings and Lord of Lords, washed the feet of his disciples. They were stunned. Peter protested. They were probably confused and humbled as the hands of their savior touched and washed their filthy feet.

Jesus' act was more than a lesson in serving with humility. His attitude and actions were in sharp contrast to the disciples' own. The meal had already begun. The disciples were already seated, with dirty feet. None of them considered washing the others' feet—or even their own. Not long before the meal began they had argued over who among them would be the greatest in the Kingdom of Heaven.

But Jesus washed their feet. Then he told them, "As you've seen me do, you do also." His message? They were to touch the filth of others in order to serve in humility and love. Hurting people hurt people and sometimes it's messy. Jesus, by His own example, taught us to get into the mess of others' lives and serve them. Sitting up late at night helping a middle school child learn math concepts that they should have learned in second grade is messy. Teaching a fourth-grader to bathe is messy. Buying door alarms because your teenager is sneaking out is messy. Staying up all night with a baby suffering from fetal alcohol syndrome is messy. Washing filthy feet is messy. Yet, our Savior did it.

As we gain entry into the lives and stories of our children. Let us humbly remember that, even in the frustration, there's beauty. We've been granted an opportunity to walk near to those whom are nearest to God's heart—the vulnerable, weak, and abandoned. As we've seen Jesus do, let us do also.

"The mercies of God are new every morning. So should ours be for our children"

There's another part of the story that's easy to miss if you're not paying attention. All of Jesus' disciples were seated at the table—including Judas. Jesus knew Judas had already betrayed him. He washed his feet anyway. I don't know about you, but it's hard for me to imagine myself washing the feet of someone that I know has betrayed me to my death. Clearly, I am not Jesus.

There will be times when your children act out. There will be times when they're selfish. There will be times when they argue with one another. There will be times when they defy you and betray your trust. In those moments, seek to imitate Jesus' attitude. This will teach your children to walk in humility, grace, patience, and love. The mercies of God are new every morning. So should ours be for our children.

Scripture Meditation: Take a few moments to read the following scriptures. Allow the Holy Spirit to speak to your heart about each of them.

John 13:3–9, 12–15 (NLT) Jesus knew that the Father had given him authority over everything and that he had come from God and would return to God. So he got up from the table, took off his robe, wrapped a towel around his waist, and poured water into a basin. Then he began to wash the disciples' feet, drying them with the towel he had around him. When Jesus came to Simon Peter, Peter said to him, "Lord, are you going to wash my feet?" Jesus replied, "You don't understand now what I am doing, but someday you will." "No," Peter protested, "You will never ever wash my feet!" Jesus replied, "Unless I wash you, you won't belong to me." Simon Peter exclaimed, "Then wash my hands and head as well, Lord, not just my feet!" … After washing their feet, he put on his robe again and sat down and asked, "Do you understand what I was doing? You call me 'Teacher' and 'Lord,' and you are right, because that's what I am. And since I, your Lord and Teacher, have washed your feet, you ought to wash each other's feet. I have given you an example to follow. Do as I have done to you.

Matthew 20:28 (NLT) For even the Son of Man came not to be served but to serve others and to give his life as a ransom for many.

Titus 1:8–9 (NLT) Rather, he must enjoy having guests in his home, and must love what is good. He must live wisely and be just. He must live a devout and disciplined life. He must have a strong belief in the trustworthy message he was taught; then he will be able to encourage others with wholesome teaching and show those who oppose it where they are wrong.

1 Corinthians 13:13 (NLT) Three things will last forever – faith, hope, and love – and the greatest of these is love.

Romans 15:1 (NLT) We who are strong must be considerate of those who are sensitive about things like this. We must not just please ourselves.

Capturing Thoughts: Throughout your adoption journey, I encourage you to capture your thoughts, fears, moments of joy, memories, and challenges. It will be a great encouragement to go back and read what you've written. You'll be surprised how much you and your family grow through your experiences.

Prayer Starter: Father, give us your heart for serving and loving unconditionally. Guide us in humility so that we can model your good and perfect love for our children.

Discussion Questions – Day 24: Washing Feet

1. Talk about a time when you've seen someone serve another with true humility. What was your reaction?

2. What messy parts of raising kids really challenge you? What do you do to move past those things?

3. Read John 13:3-10. What is the connection between letting Jesus serve us and our ability to serve others in true humility?

4. What does it mean to you that God's mercies are new every morning? How can that understanding help you as you parent?

My Journey:

(Use this space to capture your thoughts, prayers, concerns and questions)

CARRY EACH OTHER'S BURDENS,

IN THIS WAY YOU WILL FULFILL THE LAW OF CHRIST.

GALATIANS 6:2

DAY 25: BEARING BURDENS

The Greek word for burden is *bareos*. It means "something that makes an overwhelming demand, that brings sorrow or grief." There are times in our lives when we need others to come alongside us and help us carry a burden. It's in those times that we see the work of Christ in our lives through the love and care of a friend.

Our children cannot always articulate their needs. It's up to us to recognize that they can't express the pain inside except through negative behavior. It is in these times that we must rely on the discernment of the Holy Spirit to give us insight into the hidden causes of an outburst or behavior. With foster or adopted children, even a small negative behavior like telling a lie can be rooted in a web of distrust and insecurity.

If I were to do a survey of foster and adoptive parents to find out what the most difficult behaviors to deal with are, at the very top of almost everyone's list would be one. Lying. Many of the children I've known who've come from a history of trauma have issues, major issues, with lying. It took a long time for us to understand this behavior and we had many battles with our children over it. They would lie over the silliest things. Tell obvious lies and then scream and cry when we didn't believe them.

At its core, lying is a survival tactic. If our children are anything, they are true survivors. The risk a child who has been abused and abandoned takes when telling the truth and admitting that they've done something wrong is that they will be abused, abandoned, shamed or rejected. Their brains sense the pending pain and quickly create a protective response—a lie—to shield them. It makes sense. But making sense doesn't make it easy. As we've walked with our children toward healing, we've had to change our approach to lying, even sometimes ignoring the lie completely in order to focus on a deeper issue.

> **"At its core, lying is a survival tactic. If our children are anything, they are true survivors."**

Scripture is clear that we are to be gentle in the restoration of those caught in sin. Although many of the burdens our children bear are not a result of their personal sin, they are a result of the sin of another. We should be gentle in the restorative process.

We need to bear with our children's burdens, to carry them for as long as it takes—and it could take years. We are to carry their burdens in prayer, in counsel, in loving touch, in being a shoulder to cry on, in being an ear to listen to their stories, in being patient in correction and in being a loving example of Jesus Christ's unfailing love. Your time, effort, compassion, and prayers will eventually lead your children to be able to carry their own burdens before the Lord.

Scripture Meditation: Take a few moments to read the following scriptures. Allow the Holy Spirit to speak to your heart about each of them.

1 Timothy 5:8 (NLT) But those who won't care for their relatives, especially those of their own household, have denied the true faith. Such people are worse than unbelievers.

Deuteronomy 28:1–68 (please read)

Luke 10:27 (NLT) The man answered, "You must love the Lord your God with all your heart, all your soul, all your strength and all your mind." And, "Love your neighbor as yourself."

Psalm 34:18 (NLT) The Lord is close to the brokenhearted; he rescues those whose spirits are crushed.

Capturing Thoughts: Throughout your adoption journey, I encourage you to capture your thoughts, fears, moments of joy, memories, and challenges. It will be a great encouragement to go back and read what you've written. You'll be surprised how much you and your family grow through your experiences.

Prayer Starter: Father, teach us to bear the burdens of our children when they are too weak to bear them on their own. Be our constant companion and still small voice. Remind us to look more deeply at the simple behaviors and have grace, patience, and mercy.

Discussion Questions – Day 25: Bearing Burdens

1. Is your first instinct to be gentle in the restoration of those caught in sin? Why or why not?

2. Talk about someone in your life who bore your burdens. Did you recognize what he or she was doing for you at the time, or could you only see it in retrospect?

3. Read 1 Timothy 5:8. Why do you think the apostle Paul makes this connection between providing and caring for family and faith?

4. What are some of the challenges to parenting a child who lies? Are there ways you can better understand the survival behavior of lying?

My Journey:

(Use this space to capture your thoughts, prayers, concerns and questions)

TRAIN UP A CHILD IN THE WAY HE SHOULD GO,

AND WHEN HE IS OLD HE WILL NOT TURN FROM IT.

PROVERBS 22:6

DAY 26: THE PROMISE

If there is one certainty in this journey, it is this: God will keep His promises. I have reminded God of His promises often—especially when everything seems to be going wrong. I know His word does not return to me empty. We have to trust that He will see our children through their journey. In His hands, they are safe.

> **"We can convince ourselves that for Proverbs 22:6 to be true, our children must be perfect angels."**

We can convince ourselves that for Proverbs 22:6 to be true, our children must be perfect angels. This is a great stumbling block in our relationships with our kids because they feel the weight of our wanting them to be perfect so we don't feel like failures.

The Holy Spirit had to remind me of this recently. I was brooding in prayer about why we weren't seeing certain cycles of negative behavior broken in our daughter. God promised restoration and healing for her, right? The Holy Spirit asked me a simple question: "Why do you think you get to write her story?" Ouch!

In this one defining moment, I realized that everyone's testimony has to be different in order for his or her life to bring God the glory He deserves. It's not my job to write her story. I only get to play a role in it. Even now, her situation hasn't changed. My heart has, though. God hasn't shared with me his plan for her life. He has asked me to trust Him and to love her. I must remain faithful.

Hebrews 12:2 illustrates this perfectly: *"Jesus is the author and finisher of our faith."* It's easy to see that He's the author of our faith. We don't bring people to salvation. That's His job. But we forget the second part of the verse: He is the finisher too. We aren't promised that every time we put our hands to the plow we will see the harvest. We *are* promised the harvest. We can be confident that God will deliver.

As foster parents, who may only be in the life of a child for a short time, it's sometimes hard to push through the negative behaviors and trust in His promises. After all, you're probably not ever going to see the harvest, right? My friend, Sandra Stanley, calls this "parenting in the parentheses." In her own journey as a foster mom, she's discovered the beauty of investing in a child's life—no matter how long you have with him. Their time with you may be the only exposure to a loving Savior that they have in their childhood. It's often the parentheses (the important phrase that brings definition to the sentence) that has the most profound impact.

God's promises are true for *all* of our children; regardless of how long they're in our lives. We must remember not to judge our foster care experiences by the harvest our foster children bring into our lives, but by the seeds we plant in theirs.

Scripture Meditation: Take a few moments to read the following scriptures. Allow the Holy Spirit to speak to your heart about each of them.

Isaiah 55:10–11 (NLT) The rain and snow come down from the heavens and stay on the ground to water the earth. They cause grain to grow, producing seed for the farmer and bread for the hungry. It is the same with my word. I send it out, and it always produces fruit. It will accomplish all I want it to, and it will prosper everywhere I send it.

Psalm 27:13–14 (NLT) Yet I am confident I will see the Lord's goodness while I am here in the land of the living. Wait patiently for the Lord. Be brave and courageous. Yes, wait patiently for the Lord.

Jeremiah 24:7 (NLT) I will give the hearts that recognize me as the Lord. They will be my people, and I will be their God, for they will return to me wholeheartedly.

Jeremiah 31:16–18 (NLT) But now this is what the Lord says: "Do not weep any longer, for I will reward you," says the Lord. "Your children will come back to you from the distant land of the enemy. There is hope for your future," says the Lord. "Your children will come again to their own land."

1 John 5:14–15 (NLT) And we are confident that he hears us whenever we ask for anything that pleases him. And since we know he hears us when we make our requests, we also know that he will give us what we ask for.

Capturing Thoughts: Throughout your adoption journey, I encourage you to capture your thoughts, fears, moments of joy, memories, and challenges. It will be a great encouragement to go back and read what you've written. You'll be surprised how much you and your family grow through your experiences.

Prayer Starter: Father, thank you for your promises to protect our children. Draw them closer to you. Bring to harvest every seed we've sown in their lives. Grant us the patience to trust you in the difficult times. Give them the freedom to find you.

Discussion Questions – Day 26: The Promise

1. Talk about a promise that God kept in your life. How did it affect your relationship with Him?

2. Read Proverbs 22:6. As you reflect on this verse, how well does it apply to the way you were raised and to your adult life?

3. To what extent do you tend to try to be the author of your children's stories? Explain.

4. In what ways are you tempted to think that God's plans for your children's lives depend on their behavior? What practical things can you do to remind yourself that's incorrect?

My Journey:

(Use this space to capture your thoughts, prayers, concerns and questions)

AGAIN I SAY UNTO YOU, THAT IF TWO OF YOU SHALL AGREE ON EARTH AS TOUCHING ANY THING THAT THEY SHALL ASK, IT SHALL BE DONE FOR THEM OF MY FATHER, WHICH IS IN HEAVEN.

MATTHEW 18:19

DAY 27: IN AGREEMENT

If you're married, coming to an agreement on every step of the journey is essential to your success in foster care and adoption. If you're single, having two or three trusted people as wise counsel throughout the process is essential. God's Word is clear that two or more working together can do more than a lone person. It is also clear that we need wise counsel around us to help in critical decision-making.

> **"We absolutely must agree about discipline, our children's healing process, and so much more."**

To "agree" means to be in harmony. When people sing in harmony, their voices are so closely synchronized they sound like one. Parents should be one voice in prayer and one voice in parenting. Unity in Jesus Christ is one of the most powerful tools in our toolbox. We absolutely must agree about discipline, our child's healing process, and so much more. Only then can the power of God be manifested in our lives and families.

Unity protects you from kids' manipulative tactics. Sometimes when a child doesn't get the answer she wants from mom, she'll turn to dad to see if she can get what she wants. It happens all the time. Unity means parents check with each other before giving children quick answers.

There are many decisions to be made in this journey as a foster and adoptive parent. Will you foster? Will you adopt? Will you take older children? What behaviors can you parent? One parent cannot make these decisions by themselves. Both parents must be involved and must agree. If you're parenting as a single person, you shouldn't make these decisions alone. Those closest to you see far more about your personality, tolerances and capacity than you know. Allow them to speak into your process so that you can make a well-informed decision. What is your vision for your family? Does everyone agree?

With seven daughters, there's plenty of opportunity for my husband and I to disagree about something. Allowing a child permission to go here or there, buying something, issuing a consequence or giving grace on a behavioral infraction. We've learned to consult one another so that we can hear another perspective. It's not always easy because each of us always wants to believe that our solution is the right solution. However, because we consult one another regularly, we often—very often—discover that there's more to the issue than we knew. Kids are great at playing adults against one another. Somehow, regardless of upbringing, they have innate ability to sense when they can get something out of one adult and not the other—and they love to practice that skill.

Standing together is easier than standing alone. In times when one of you is weak, the other is strong. Knowing that you always have someone to talk to, vent to, cry with, and make decisions with leads to a more peaceful household and a more successful foster and adoptive journey.

Scripture Meditation: Take a few moments to read the following scriptures. Allow the Holy Spirit to speak to your heart about each of them.

Deuteronomy 32:30 (NLT) How could one person chase a thousand of them, and two people put then thousand to flight, unless their Rock had sold them, unless the Lord had given them up.

Genesis 11:5–6 (NLT) But the Lord came down to look at the city and the tower the people were building. "Look!" he said. "The people are united, and they all speak the same language. After this, nothing they set out to do will be impossible for them!"

Psalm 133:1 (NLT) How wonderful and pleasant it is when brothers live together in harmony.

Amos 3:3 (NLT) Can two people walk together without agreeing on the direction?

Ephesians 4:15-16 (NLT) Instead, we will speak the truth in love, growing in every way more and more like Christ, who is the head of his body, the church. He makes the whole body fit together perfectly. As each part does its own special work, it helps the other parts grow, so that the whole body is healthy and growing and full of love.

Capturing Thoughts: Throughout your adoption journey, I encourage you to capture your thoughts, fears, moments of joy, memories, and challenges. It will be a great encouragement to go back and read what you've written. You'll be surprised how much you and your family grow through your experiences.

Prayer Starter: Father, help us become one in you. Help us to accept your will concerning our children. Give us the wisdom to stand together. Grant us agreement with one another according to your word. Thank you for your promise of protection, guidance, and wisdom in unity.

Discussion Questions – Day 27: In Agreement

1. When you were a child, did you ever try to play one of your parents against the other? How well did it work?

2. Talk about an area in your life where it's difficult for you and your spouse to agree. What approaches do you take to manage that tension?

3. Who do you turn to for wise counsel? If you don't currently rely on anyone, what are the names of two or three people you can reach out to?

4. What steps do you need to take to ensure that you are united when it comes to caring for children? What can this group do to support you?

My Journey:

(Use this space to capture your thoughts, prayers, concerns and questions)

DO NOT BE AFRAID OR DISCOURAGED BECAUSE OF THIS VAST ARMY. FOR THE
BATTLE IS NOT YOURS, BUT GOD'S . . . YOU WILL NOT HAVE TO FIGHT THIS
BATTLE. TAKE UP YOUR POSITIONS; STAND FIRM AND SEE THE DELIVERANCE
THE LORD WILL GIVE YOU.

2 CHRONICLES 20:15,17

DAY 28: FAITH'S STAND

In Chronicles, King Jehoshaphat pours out his heart to God. He asks for
God's help against a mighty foe. Many times, I've felt what Jehoshaphat must
have felt at that moment: scared and defenseless against a mighty foe. In my
case the mighty foe was a runaway child, a suicide attempt, a teen pregnancy,
or an angry outburst from one of my children.

When we face a parenting battle, God answers our prayers the same way
he answered Jehoshaphat's: *"The battle is not yours, but God's...You will not have
to fight this battle. Take up your positions; stand firm and see the deliverance the Lord will
give you."* In those moments when we're at our weakest, God stands beside
us, whispering, *"Don't let go . . . don't give up . . . I've got this . . . trust me . . . stand
firm, my child."*

In 1 Peter 5:8–9, we're given our marching orders: "Be self-controlled and
alert. Your enemy the devil prowls around like a roaring lion looking for
someone to devour. Resist him, standing firm in the faith... " Everything in
us may be battle-worn and tired, but we must control ourselves, stay calm,
and be alert to the tactics of the enemy. We are in a war for the affections of
our children. Our adversary knows that we are the sentinels at the gate. If

he's going to gain full access to their hearts, he must wear us down and shake us from our posts.

> **"We are in a war for the affections of our children. If he's going to gain access to their hearts, he must wear us down and shake us from our posts."**

Not too long ago, we suffered a major blow in our parenting. Three of our children were in behavioral crisis at the same time. I have never felt so exhausted and drained in my life. In those dark days, I literally felt the presence of the enemy, up close, as if he were breathing down my neck. For the first time in my life, I had no words to pray. I spent night after night crying.

In desperation, I reached out to a select few of my family and friends and let them in on the whole ugly truth. Suddenly, an army of believers was fighting with me and for me. The words that I didn't have—they did. The prayers that I couldn't pray—they could. The problems didn't end immediately, but my burden lifted and I found the strength to stand firm in my faith. On my own, I believe I would have surely crumbled. Thankfully, the Holy Spirit prompted me to call in an army. Looking back, I see the mighty hand of God at work. Others who were praying also began talking with my kids, mentoring them, comforting them and guiding them.

For me it was an Aaron and Hur moment (Exodus 17:11&12). I was too tired to keep up the fight, so God sent in others to lift up my arms so that spiritual forces I could not see would be defeated.

Let's continually remind ourselves that He is the beginning and the end, going before us to pave the way and coming behind us to protect us.

Scripture Meditation: Take a few moments to read the following scriptures. Allow the Holy Spirit to speak to your heart about each of them.

> **1 Thessalonians 5:18** (NLT) Be thankful in all circumstances, for this is God's will for you who belong to Christ Jesus.

> **Exodus 14:13** (NLT) But Moses told the people, "Don't be afraid. Just stand still and watch the Lord rescue you today. The Egyptians you see today will never be seen again."

> **Psalm 20:7–8** (NLT) Some nations boast of their chariots and horses, but we boast in the name of the Lord our God. Those nations will fall down and collapse, but we will rise up and stand firm.

> **Psalm 40:2** (NLT) He lifted me out of the pit of despair, out of the mud and the mire. He set my feet on solid ground and steadied me as I walked along.

Capturing Thoughts: Throughout your adoption journey, I encourage you to capture your thoughts, fears, moments of joy, memories, and challenges. It will be a great encouragement to go back and read what you've written. You'll be surprised how much you and your family grow through your experiences.

Prayer Starter: Father, thank you for your protection and favor. We know you've called us and will equip us. We know you will establish our steps. Remind us that you go to battle on our behalf and that our children's issues are yours to heal. We are your hands and feet.

Discussion Questions – Day 28: Faith's Stand

1. Talk about a time when you were out of your depth and forced to rely entirely on God. What did that experience do for your relationship with your heavenly Father?

2. To what extent have you considered the inevitable exhaustion that comes with parenting as you committed to adoption or foster care? What strategies have you or can you put in place to combat that exhaustion?

3. Read 1 Peter 5:8-9. When it comes to raising children, what do you think it means to be self-controlled and alert?

4. Today's devotion says, "Let's continually remind ourselves that He is the beginning and the end, going before us to pave the way and coming behind us to protect us." What are some practical ways you can remind yourself on a daily basis? How can this group help you?

My Journey:

(Use this space to capture your thoughts, prayers, concerns and questions)

FOR HE CHOSE US IN HIM BEFORE THE CREATION OF THE WORLD TO

BE HOLY AND BLAMELESS IN HIS SIGHT. IN LOVE, HE PREDESTINED US FOR

ADOPTION TO SONSHIP THROUGH JESUS CHRIST, IN ACCORDANCE

WITH HIS PLEASURE AND WILL.

EPHESIANS 1:4–5

DAY 29: YOU ARE ADOPTED

We were once lost and without hope. Then God, through Jesus, adopted us and called us sons and daughters. He made us joint heirs with Christ. We now have eternal security in heaven, a full inheritance in Christ Jesus. Our status as sons and daughters of the most high God is assured for eternity. He will never leave us or forsake us. He will never quit on us. He will never kick us out of His family. He will never deny us entrance into heaven. He will never stop loving us. What great peace and comfort that brings! No matter what we do, Jesus' love is ours. We can turn to Him to lift us up and care for us.

> **"Nothing transforms a child's heart like a feeling of belonging. Having parents who believe in, love, and invest in him everyday changes his life."**

The assurance God gives us is similar to what we give our wounded children: belonging, hope, unconditional love, and acceptance. Nothing transforms a child's heart like a feeling of belonging. Having parents who believe in, love, and invest in him every day changes his life. Just as we say,

"I don't know what my life would be like without Jesus," there will come a day when your children will say, "I don't know what my life would be like without my mom and dad." It may not happen tomorrow, but it *will* happen.

A friend of mine, Dennis Russell, spoke a promise to me once that I've held onto for years. As an adoptee himself, he has a unique understanding of the heart and mind of adopted children. We were sitting on the back of a bus and I had shared some difficulty we were having with one of our daughters. She was at a place where everything we did for her was being rejected. Whether she really wanted it or not, she was shunning it. Clothes, outings, and spending time with family—nothing would satisfy. Dennis looked at me and said, "Pam, there's no way at her age that she can see what you're trying to do. Right now she's just hurting and mad. But one day, she will say thank you. With tears in her eyes, she will understand the depth of your love for her. You just have to be able to stick with her until that day." Those words changed me. They gave me hope.

If the prize of our parenting is gratitude in the moment, we will certainly miss the greater picture. I've heard "thank you" from many of my now adult daughters, but the words weren't as sweet as I'd once imagined them to be. The sweeter thing is the memories I have of the fight. Standing with them in the darkness drew us closer. That closeness is much better than any words could ever be.

As we model Jesus Christ and His unconditional love to our children, their spirits will resound with joy. God's transforming power will be at work in their lives. Reminding ourselves that we share in their adoption through Jesus keeps our hearts and minds focused on the prize of heaven.

Scripture Meditation: Take a few moments to read the following scriptures. Allow the Holy Spirit to speak to your heart about each of them.

Romans 8:15, 23 (NLT) So you have not received a spirit that makes you fearful slaves. Instead, you received God's Spirit when he adopted you as his own children. Now we call him, "Abba, Father." … And we believers also groan, even though we have the Holy Spirit with us as a foretaste of future glory, for we long for our bodies to be released from sin and suffering. We, too, wait with eager hope for the day when God will give us our full rights as his adopted children, including the new bodies he has promised us.

John 1:12 (NLT) But to all who believed him and accepted him, he gave the right to become children of God.

1 John 3:1–2 (NLT) See how very much our Father loves us, for he calls us his children, and that is what we are! But the people who belong to this world don't recognize that we are God's children because they do not know Him.

Galatians 4:4–6 (NLT) But when the right time came, God sent his Son, born of a woman, subject to the law. God sent him to buy freedom for us who were slaves to the law, so that he could adopt us as his very own children. And because we are his children, God has sent the Spirit of his Son into our hearts, prompting us to call out, "Abba, Father."

Capturing Thoughts: Throughout your adoption journey, I encourage you to capture your thoughts, fears, moments of joy, memories, and challenges. It will be a great encouragement to go back and read what you've written. You'll be surprised how much you and your family grow through your experiences.

Prayer Starter: Father, thank you for calling me your child. Thank you for accepting me as I am in all my human weakness. Remind me that you love and accept me. Help me to love and accept my children.

Discussion Questions – Day 29: You Are Adopted

1. Talk about a relationship in which you experience belonging, hope, unconditional love, and acceptance. What does that relationship do for the quality of your life?

2. Read Ephesians 1:4-5. How does it strike you that God chose you before the creation of the world? How does it affect the way you view Him?

3. Today's devotion says, "Nothing transforms a child's heart like a feeling of belonging." Do you agree? Why or why not?

4. What are some practical ways you can cultivate a sense of belonging in the lives of your children?

My Journey:

(Use this space to capture your thoughts, prayers, concerns and questions)

ESTHER 4:14B

DAY 30: FOR SUCH A TIME AS THIS

The book of Esther tells the story of a beautiful orphaned girl raised by her uncle Mordecai. She finds favor with the King of Persia and becomes his Queen. There's one thing the King doesn't know about Esther: she's Jewish. The King issues a decree that all Jews living in Persia are to be killed. Esther has a dilemma. She can defend the cause of her people and risk dying at the hand of her husband or keep quiet and watch her people die. She asks her uncles advice. He says, *"For if you keep silent at this time, relief and deliverance will rise for the Jews from another place, but you and your father's house will perish. And who knows whether you have not come to the kingdom for such a time as this?"* Esther summons the courage to face the King and her people are saved. She truly was born for such a time as this.

The truth is, God is the defender of the fatherless (Isaiah 1:17). He will deliver and defend them, with or without us. But who knows whether we have not been called into the kingdom for this? God doesn't need us, he chose us. What a privilege and honor that is. I hold the gift of being the healing hands of Jesus in my children's life with open hands. Honoring God and acknowledging that He could use anyone, yet He selected me.

Just like Esther, we have no indication of what the final outcome will be, so we must summon the courage the face the issues of every day.

We are here for *such a time as this*—to set our children free. This is Jesus' call to be His hands and feet to the fatherless.

> **"Love your children with abandon. Bear with them in patience. Lay down your life so they may find theirs."**

As you set out on your journey, let me encourage you, thank you, and challenge you to be all God has called you to be. Love your children with abandon. Bear with them in patience. Lay down your life so they may find theirs.

In every day, find beauty. In every conflict, find peace. In every moment, make memories. You never know what tomorrow will hold. But you can know that the Maker of tomorrow holds you—and your children—today.

Your family will increase. You will face many hurdles and experience much joy along the way. I pray that, through you, your children may know their heavenly Father. My prayer is that they may also become the hands and feet of Jesus, bringing deliverance to those they come in contact with.

Thank you for journeying with me for the last 30 days. I pray that you've discovered a God whose heart burns for the fatherless.

Scripture Meditation: Take a few moments to read the following scriptures. Allow the Holy Spirit to speak to your heart about each of them.

Proverbs 19:21 (NLT) You can make plans, but the Lord's purpose will prevail.

Exodus 9:16 (NLT) But I have spared you for a purpose – to show you my power and to spread my fame throughout the Earth.

Jeremiah 29:11 (NLT) "For I know the plans I have for you," says the Lord. "They are plans for good and not for disaster, to give you a future and a hope."

Philippians 2:5 (NLT) You must have the same attitude that Christ Jesus had.

Romans 8:28 (NLT) And we know that God causes everything to work together for the good of those who love God and are called according to his purpose for them.

Capturing Thoughts: Throughout your adoption journey, I encourage you to capture your thoughts, fears, moments of joy, memories, and challenges. It will be a great encouragement to go back and read what you've written. You'll be surprised how much you and your family grow through your experiences.

Prayer Starter: Father, thank you for calling us. This is our time to make a difference in the lives of our children so they can become disciples of Jesus. We're honored that you chose us *for such a time as this.*

Discussion Questions – Day 30: For Such a Time As This

1. Read Proverbs 19:21. In what ways has God surprised you with the plans He's had for your life? In general, how have His plans for you compared with your plans?

2. As you think about the story of Esther, how does it inspire or challenge how you view your children's potential?

3. Today's devotion says, "God doesn't need us, he chose us. What a privilege and honor that is. I hold the gift of being the healing hands of Jesus in my children's life with open hands. Honoring God and acknowledging that He could use anyone, yet He selected me." How does knowing that God handpicked you for this journey make you feel? What are some things you can do to remind yourself of this truth, especially when things get tough?

4. What are some challenges you face in trusting God to change others' lives *through* you? What are some practical things you can do to address those challenges?

My Journey:

(Use this space to capture your thoughts, prayers, concerns and questions)

ABOUT THE AUTHOR

Pam Parish is the president and founder of Connections Homes, an Atlanta-based nonprofit organization focused on providing family-based home environments where adolescents with difficult pasts and uncertain futures can connect, grow and belong. She and her husband, Steve, were high school sweethearts. More than two decades later, they are still best friends. At the time of this writing, they have seven daughters: Katya Grace, Kelsey Joy, Elizabeth Yeaune Harang (Jesus' blessing and love), Seara Serenity, Charlie Selah, Kristan Faith, and Heather Hope. They also have three grandsons, Juan, Jayden and Junior, and one granddaughter, Adrianna. Pam is a foster care and adoption advocate, public speaker, trainer, and family crisis mentor.

ABOUT SANDRA STANLEY

Sandra Stanley is married to her best friend Andy (senior pastor of North Point Ministries) and resides in Atlanta, GA. Mom to Andrew, Garrett and Allie. She's also a foster mom who is learning, stretching and trying to figure out how to best love on little hearts that need healing. Through North Point's Fostering Together ministry, the Stanley's have served as foster parents, respite partners and as support and mentor participants. Sandra blogs at sandrastanley.com about faith, family and fostering. You can follow her on Twitter @sandrawstanley.

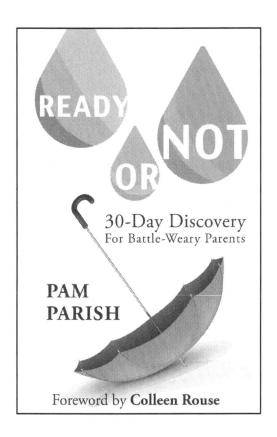

Ready or Not *for Battle-Weary Parents*

Book Two in the Ready or Not Series for Foster and Adoptive Families

From the moment a child enters our life, parenting is a tough job. It's even harder when a child is struggling with difficult behaviors—defiance, rejection, running away, drug addiction, sexual misconduct, criminal activity, attachment issues, rage and beyond. Parenting a child in crisis leaves parents worn out from exhaustion, frustration and fear.

God doesn't leave us, even in the midst of our fears, failures and fatigue. In this powerful second book in the Ready or Not Series, you will be encouraged and challenged as a battle-weary parent. Ready or Not, 30-Day Discovery for Battle-Weary Parents is an essential tool for anyone struggling to walk with their kids through crisis.

To stay up-to-date on the *Ready or Not Series* visit <u>readyornotresources.com</u>

Family Photo Credit: Kelly Hopkins

Connect With Pam Online

@pamparish   facebook.com/pamparish

pinterest.com/pamparish   google.com/+pamparish

Pam also shares inspiration for foster and adoptive parents on her blog: **pamparish.com**.

To inquire about having Pam speak at your church, agency or conference e-mail <u>booking@pamparish.com</u> or visit pamparish.com/contact.

Speaking & Training

Healing Power of Words

Our words can significantly impact the progress of our children's healing journey. Learn how to use your words to bring healing and promote connection in your relationship with your kids.

Belonging Matters

Everyone needs to belong to someone. At the core of identity in family and life is a healthy sense belonging. Learn how to foster a sense of belonging in foster & adoptive children.

Ready or Not

Straight-forward and honest discussion about the ups and downs of foster care and adoption. Pam will often speak with several of our daughters from both a birth child and foster/adopted child viewpoint.

Empowered to Connect

Pam and her husband, Steve, are certified Empowered to Connect trainers. They understand, teach and promote the philosophies of ETC and Trust-Based Parenting.

Scripture has much to say about about orphans. Here's a list of verses that mention the fatherless and orphan.

Exodus 22:22-24

Do not take advantage of a widow or an **orphan**. If you do and they cry out to me, I will certainly hear their cry. My anger will be aroused, and I will kill you with the sword; your wives will become widows and your children **fatherless**.

Deuteronomy 10:18

He defends the cause of the **fatherless** and the widow, and loves the alien, giving him food and clothing.

Deuteronomy 14:29

So that the Levites (who have no allotment or inheritance of their own) and the aliens, the **fatherless** and the widows who live in your towns may come and eat and be satisfied, and so that the LORD your God may bless you in all the work of your hands.

Deuteronomy 16:11

And rejoice before the LORD your God at the place he will choose as a dwelling for his Name—you, your sons and daughters, your menservants and maidservants, the Levites in your towns, and the aliens, the **fatherless** and the widows living among you.

Deuteronomy 16:14

Be joyful at your Feast--you, your sons and daughters, your menservants and maidservants, and the Levites, the aliens, the **fatherless** and the widows who live in your towns.

Deuteronomy 24:17

Do not deprive the alien or the **fatherless** of justice, or take the cloak of the widow as a pledge.

Deuteronomy 24:19-21

When you are harvesting in your field and you overlook a sheaf, do not go back to get it. Leave it for the alien, the **fatherless** and the widow, so that the LORD your God may bless you in all the work of your hands. When you beat the olives from your trees, do not go over the branches a second time. Leave what remains for the alien, the **fatherless** and the widow. When you harvest the grapes in your vineyard, do not go over the vines again. Leave what remains for the alien, the **fatherless** and the widow.

Deuteronomy 26:12 -13

When you have finished setting aside a tenth of all your produce in the third year, the year of the tithe, you shall give it to the Levite, the alien, the **fatherless** and the widow, so that they may eat in your towns and be satisfied. Then say to the LORD your God: "I have removed from my house the sacred portion and have given it to the Levite, the alien, the **fatherless** and the widow, according to all you commanded. I have not turned aside from your commands nor have I forgotten any of them.

Deuteronomy 27:19

"Cursed is the man who withholds justice from the alien, the **fatherless** or the widow." Then all the people shall say, "Amen!"

Job 6:27

You would even cast lots for the **fatherless** and barter away your friend.

Job 22:7-11

You gave no water to the weary and you withheld food from the hungry, though you were a powerful man, owning land-- an honored man, living on it.

And you sent widows away empty-handed and broke the strength of the **fatherless**. That is why snares are all around you, why sudden peril terrifies you, why it is so dark you cannot see, and why a flood of water covers you.

Job 24:2-4

Men move boundary stones; they pasture flocks they have stolen. They drive away the **orphan's** donkey and take the widow's ox in pledge. They thrust the needy from the path and force all the poor of the land into hiding.

Job 24:9

The **fatherless** child is snatched from the breast; the infant of the poor is seized for a debt.

Job 29:11-12

Whoever heard me spoke well of me, and those who saw me commended me, because I rescued the poor who cried for help, and the **fatherless** who had none to assist him.

Job 31:16-18

"If I have denied the desires of the poor or let the eyes of the widow grow weary, if I have kept my bread to myself, not sharing it with the **fatherless** - but from my youth I reared him as would a father, and from my birth I guided the widow.

Job 31:21-22

If I have raised my hand against the **fatherless**, knowing that I had influence in court, then let my arm fall from the shoulder, let it be broken off at the joint.

Psalm 10:14

But you, O God, do see trouble and grief; you consider it to take it in hand. The victim commits himself to you; you are the helper of the **fatherless**.

Psalm 10:17-18

You hear, O LORD, the desire of the afflicted; you encourage them, and you listen to their cry, defending the **fatherless** and the oppressed, in order that man, who is of the earth, may terrify no more.

Psalm 68:5-6

A father to the **fatherless**, a defender of widows, is God in his holy dwelling. God sets the lonely in families, he leads forth the prisoners with singing; but the rebellious live in a sun-scorched land.

Psalm 82:3-4

Defend the cause of the weak and **fatherless**; maintain the rights of the poor and oppressed. Rescue the weak and needy; deliver them from the hand of the wicked.

Psalm 94:6

They slay the widow and the alien; they murder the **fatherless**.

Psalm 146:9

The LORD watches over the alien and sustains the **fatherless** and the widow, but he frustrates the ways of the wicked.

Proverbs 23:10-11

Do not move an ancient boundary stone or encroach on the fields of the **fatherless**, for their Defender is strong; he will take up their case against you.

Isaiah 1:17

Learn to do right! Seek justice, encourage the oppressed. Defend the cause of the **fatherless**, plead the case of the widow.

Isaiah 1:23

Our rulers are rebels, companions of thieves; they all love bribes and chase after gifts. They do not defend the cause of the **fatherless**; the widow's case does not come before them.

Isaiah 9:17

Therefore the Lord will take no pleasure in the young men, nor will he pity the **fatherless** and widows, for everyone is ungodly and wicked, every mouth speaks vileness. Yet for all this, his anger is not turned away, his hand is still upraised.

Isaiah 10:1-2

Woe to those who make unjust laws, to those who issue oppressive decrees, to deprive the poor of their rights and withhold justice from the oppressed of my people, making widows their prey and robbing the **fatherless**.

Jeremiah 5:27-29

Like cages full of birds, their houses are full of deceit; they have become rich and powerful and have grown fat and sleek. Their evil deeds have no limit; they do not plead the case of the **fatherless** to win it, they do not defend the rights of the poor. Should I not punish them for this?" declares the LORD. "Should I not avenge myself on such a nation as this?"

Jeremiah 7:5-7

If you really change your ways and your actions and deal with each other justly, if you do not oppress the alien, the **fatherless** or the widow and do not shed innocent blood in this place, and if you do not follow other gods to your own harm, then I will let you live in this place, in the land I gave your forefathers for ever and ever.

Jeremiah 22:3

This is what the LORD says: Do what is just and right. Rescue from the hand of his oppressor the one who has been robbed. Do no wrong or violence to the alien, the **fatherless** or the widow, and do not shed innocent blood in this place.

Jeremiah 49:11
Leave your **orphans**; I will protect their lives. Your widows too can trust in me.

Ezekiel 22:7
In you they have treated father and mother with contempt; in you they have oppressed the alien and mistreated the **fatherless** and the widow.

Hosea 14:3
Assyria cannot save us; we will not mount war-horses. We will never again say 'Our gods' to what our own hands have made, for in you the **fatherless** find compassion.

Zechariah 7:10
Do not oppress the widow or the **fatherless**, the alien or the poor. In your hearts do not think evil of each other.

Malachi 3:5
So I will come near to you for judgment. I will be quick to testify against sorcerers, adulterers and perjurers, against those who defraud laborers of their wages, who oppress the widows and the **fatherless**, and deprive aliens of justice, but do not fear me," says the LORD Almighty.

John 14:18
I will not leave you as **orphans**; I will come to you.